Cuthbert Heath

Cuthbert Heath

Maker of the Modern Lloyd's of London

Antony Brown

David & Charles
Newton Abbot London

© C. E. Heath & Co. Limited, 1980

This book was designed and produced by
George Rainbird Limited,
36 Park Street,
London W1Y 4DE

Brown, Antony
  Cuthbert Heath.
  1. Heath, Cuthbert   2. Insurance – Great Britain
  – Biography
  368'.0092'4   HG8597
ISBN: 0-7153-7942-9

House Editor: Elizabeth Blair
Designer: Gail Engert

Printed and bound by W. S. Cowell Ltd. Ipswich

HALF TITLE *The Times Grand Prix*
for financial advertising awarded to C. E.
Heath & Co Limited in 1977

FRONTISPIECE A view of the Room at Lloyd's

Contents

Colour Plates

The page numbers given are those opposite the colour plates.

THE QUEEN'S AWARD FOR
EXPORT ACHIEVEMENT
1978

Preface

Perhaps surprisingly, there is still only a relatively small amount of general literature on the subject of insurance, and this book is aimed to give the ordinary reader some account of the industry's most important pioneer in its modern, if not its entire, history. While I would hope that the story of Cuthbert Heath will be of interest to those engaged in the markets which he did so much to create, I should stress that the book is above all designed for readers who are, like myself, in no sense insurance experts.

Any book of this kind must depend on the co-operation of a large number of people, and I must first express my gratitude to Mr Frank Holland, the chairman of C. E. Heath and Co., who originally proposed the project. I have also been greatly helped by the enthusiasm and kindness of several members of the Heath family, and I must especially thank Lady Claud Hamilton. She has been a fount of enthusiasm as well as a mine of information on everything to do with her father, and I am most grateful to her for her encouragement and the many hours she has spent in talking to me. I must also thank Mrs Joan Sarll for much information and many perceptive insights, and for her help and hospitality at Coldharbour. Mr Mark Heath was kind enough to allow me to see the unpublished memoirs of his uncle, Philip Heath, and other family records, and I must also thank Mrs Edwin Wood for some most interesting recollections.

The help I have received from members of Heaths' present staff has been unstinting, but I must especially thank Mr John Mikami, and Mr Brian Thompson who has been a resourceful, understanding and more than patient companion through all stages of the book's preparation. I would also particularly like to record my thanks to Mr David Barham for his helpful guidance.

I have been fortunate in being able to draw on the experience and memories of several members of Heaths' staff who are now retired, and I must especially single out Mr Eric Squire, who has been an invaluable mentor on many stages of the company's history. I am most grateful to him not only for his comments and criticisms at many stages of the writing, but also for his lucid exposition of the more esoteric areas of insurance practice.

Mr George Thomson gave me a great many interesting recollections both of Cuthbert Heath himself and of the company in more

PREVIOUS PAGE The San Francisco earthquake, 1906. The Heath syndicate, as leaders on Lloyd's earthquake policies, faced enormous losses. Cuthbert Heath simply sent a cable to his San Francisco agent: 'Pay all our policy-holders in full irrespective of the terms of their policies,' and thereby made the reputation of Lloyd's in the USA

OPPOSITE In April 1978 The Queen's Award for Export Achievement was conferred upon C. E. Heath & Co Limited. The citation referred to the fact that over a three-year period the Company's overseas earnings had more than doubled recent years, and I am deeply indebted to him for his kindness. Mr Dick Erlebach has been a particularly valuable guide to the events of the 1960s and 1970s, and I am especially grateful to him for allowing me to use his own notes on the history of C. E. Heath & Co. Mr Sidney Smith has also allowed me to draw on his great knowledge of the company, and I am most grateful to him. Others who have helped me include Mr Robert Sprinks, Mr Charles Gould, Mr Robert Langley, Mr John Cope, Mr Bruce Miller and the late Mr William Rogers. Mr Percy Holford was an admirable guide to the history of jewellery insurance and also drew my attention to some very useful written sources. I am particularly grateful to Mr Lewis Angel for some most interesting claims stories, as well as for much background information.

I should also like to thank a number of people outside Heaths, including Lord Cobbold, and Mr Adrian Palmer of Chicago who was most kind in giving me a lengthy interview. Mr Michael Dane, formerly of the Excess Company, was kind enough to allow me to use the company's archives. Mr A. E. Dunster of the Guardian Royal Exchange was a most interesting guide to the old Lloyd's Rooms in the Royal Exchange Building, and I am very grateful to him. I am also much indebted to Mr Duncan Stewart, Mr S. H. van Geuns and Mr Marcel Kortenbout. Among those who knew Cuthbert Heath at Leith Hill, I am grateful to Mrs George Salt, Dr Hal Boake, and to Mr Leslie Jones, the present owner of Anstie, for his courtesy on several visits. Mr Frith was kind enough to show me round Brighton College.

The Chairman and Committee of Lloyd's have been most kind in allowing me to use the Lloyd's archives, and I am particularly grateful for their permission to quote from the history of Lloyd's by D. E. W. Gibb, which remains essential reading for any student of this subject. Mr Terence Dinan, the Librarian of Lloyd's, helped to clear up a tricky point on Cuthbert Heath's underwriting, and Mr Desmond Rewell of Lloyd's Non-Marine Underwriters' Association was most kind in allowing me to see the Association's early minutebooks. I must also thank Mr Derek Hepworth, for his generosity in allowing me to have access to his own research material, and for much other help and guidance. I am also grateful to Mr David Wainwright, the historian of Broadwoods, for allowing me to use his own notes relating to Cuthbert Heath.

My thanks are also due to Mr Adrian Lee, the Librarian of the Chartered Insurance Institute, and to my editor, Elizabeth Blair. My secretary, Mrs Diana Cookson, has been helpful and knowledgeable as always, and I must once again thank Mrs Liliana Archibald for an index which is lively as well as comprehensive.

Apart from the invaluable Gibb, I have made extensive use of the earlier history of Lloyd's by Wright and Fayle. Among other books, I would especially mention Professor George Clayton's authoritative but highly readable *British Insurance* (Elek 1971), while another useful source has been the late Harold E. Raynes' *History of British Insurance* (Pitman 1964). Among earlier works, W. A. Dinsdale's *History of Accident Insurance in Great Britain* (Stone and Cox 1954) remains a mine of detailed information, and G. J. Emmanuel's *Memories of Lloyd's 1890–1937* (privately printed, 1937) and Elia Shenkman's *Insurance Against Credit Risks* (P. S. King, 1935) have been very useful guides to their specific subjects. I have also drawn on the Revd. Nelson Bitton's monograph of Arthur Burns (Priory Press) which Burns' grandson, Mr Donald Burns, was kind enough to lend me. *The Records of the Heath Family*, arranged by the late George Heath and privately printed in two volumes in 1913 and 1920, were of inestimable help on the early chapters, and I have also drawn on Sarah Heath's *The Story of the Gambiers* (St Clements' Press 1924). The anonymously-written *Irons in the Fire: A History of Matthews Wrightson* has also been a valuable source on Cuthbert Heath's early underwriting.

CHAPTER ONE

Family Group

No observer of English social history can fail to notice the impact made on it by family tradition. Through the centuries the famous names stand out like recurring guideposts – Cecils, Huxleys, Stracheys, Darwins. Not all have been so famous or necessarily highborn: through the eighteenth and nineteenth centuries, especially, the social life of England was enormously enriched by families in which, though many came from humble origins, it was almost a point of honour to produce a bishop, an admiral, a scholar in each successive generation.

It was such a tradition that Cuthbert Heath was born to inherit. As a small boy at Anstie Grange, on the southern slopes of Leith Hill in Surrey, he must often have gazed at the family portraits, the formidable features of ancestors who had been Royal Academicians, admirals and lawyers.

The family motto would have had its edge of challenge too. 'What we are', it ran, 'not whence we came.' Then what, he may have wondered, exactly was he? At nine or ten he was probably conscious of being a little shy and withdrawn, of not being particularly outstanding in his school work. Certainly he was aware, too, of being somewhat handicapped by deafness. If he could see a place for himself in the hierarchy of Heaths at all, it would be in the Navy: not only was his father a famous admiral, but his godfather, Sir William Eden, one of the lords of Admiralty, had given him a nomination for the Navy at his christening.

Meanwhile there were pleasanter, less daunting things to think of than the future. There were birdsnesting trips with his brothers, shooting over his father's fields, and riding over Duke's Warren, the upper slopes of Leith Hill from which the view stretched across the blue distances of Sussex to the South Downs.

'What we are, not whence we came.' Where in fact had the Heath tradition stemmed from?

PREVIOUS PAGE View over the Surrey Hills for which Cuthbert Heath had the greatest affection

The first Heath of whom we have any knowledge is Joseph Heath, who kept a bookshop in South Parade, Nottingham, around the 1740s. Thus in the first sentence of its history two aspects of the family tradition stand revealed. Joseph Heath flourished more than half a century before Napoleon made his famous but ambivalent

comment on the English nation, but already small shopkeepers like him were laying the foundations of the country's coming century of commercial success. And the second point is that he was a man of culture, for books are a commodity that no one sells unless he loves them.

There was a third quality in Joseph Heath that would have been very recognizable to his great-great-great-grandson. He must have had a pioneering instinct in business, for he was one of the first people to see the possibilities of lending libraries. Some time before 1748, and apparently in association with his son, also named Joseph, he opened the first in Nottingham, with a catalogue of:

Instructive and Entertaining Books, consisting of 600 Volumes in History, Lives, Memoirs, Voyages, Travels, Romances, Novels, Poetry, Plays, Miscellanies &c. Let out to be read, by the Quarter, Month, Week, &c. By Joseph Heath, Junior, Bookseller, Binder and Stationer. Next door to the Boot and Shoe, in the Market Place, Nottingham.

Handbill published by Joseph Heath of Nottingham. He laid the foundations of the Heath family traditions of culture and commercial acumen

Being a very Choice Collection of its Kind; the Whole Collection being
Letter'd, many of them New, neatly Bound, and all in good condition,
with the Prices fix'd to each book. Also great variety of single Plays, at
4d. and 6d. each; with Plays and Pamphlets to Let out to Read, at One
Penny each. Likewise new Entertaining Books, &c, as soon as Publish'd
either to Read or at the Lowest Prices, and the full Value given for
Libraries or Parcels of books. He also takes in Subscriptions for the
Gentlemen's, London, Universal and British Magazines. And all other
Monthly and Weekly Papers. Catalogues to be had Gratis at his Shop.

After this intriguing glimpse of the range of Nottingham's liter-
ary tastes, Joseph vanishes from view. The only other thing we
know about him is that he died some time before 1750, leaving three
sons and a daughter, Hannah. Of the sons, Joseph seems to have
followed his father in the bookshop, while George, the youngest,
also followed in his father's footsteps – at least closely enough to
become apprenticed in 1738 to a bookbinder in Duck Lane, Nottingham. His apprenticeship served, he moved to London where he kept
a stationer's shop in Butcher Row off Newgate Street.
    Here, in 1757, was born his son James, Historical Engraver to the
King, and the first of the formidable line whose portraits the young
Cuthbert Heath must have gazed at in the galleries at Anstie.

James is the first Heath of whom we know any detailed facts. He
was apprenticed to Collyer the engraver in Plough Court, Fetter
Lane, when he was fourteen, and his rise to fame was closely linked
to that of Thomas Stothard, who has been described as the most
prolific book-illustrator in history.
    From their early days the two were friends. When Stothard was
commissioned to illustrate, for example, the latest novel by Field-
ing, Richardson or Smollett, it was invariably Heath who would
engrave his work. Among their most successful vehicles was the
hugely popular *Novelists' Magazine*, first published in 1779; more
than half a century later, wrote one morning newspaper, its twenty-
two volumes remained 'a monument to the supremacy of the genius
and skill of Heath and Stothard.'
    But James Heath's tumultuous talents were not to be confined to
mere book-illustration. Soon he was at work on huge designs, lavish
and grandiose battle-scenes by Benjamin West and portraits or full-
length paintings of such contemporary celebrities as Washington
and Pitt. In 1791, he was elected an Assistant Engraver of the Royal
Academy and when, three years later, he was made Historical Engraver to King George III, it was the salutation of a talent prized,
said the *Morning Chronicle*, 'in all the principal cities of Europe'.
    Cuthbert Heath, when his time came, was to show a prodigious

flair for making money. Perhaps it was a trait that he inherited from the engraver, for the popularity of James' early bookplates for *Bell's Poets* and the *Novelists' Magazine*, according to one – perhaps envious – contemporary memoir,

> afforded Heath an opportunity of turning his talent to account, of which he did not fail to profit. He constantly employed a considerable number of assistants, from whose labours he derived great pecuniary advantages, and willingly sacrificed a portion of his reputation as an artist, to his desire of becoming a rich man.

The comment may or may not have been unfair, but in other ways James Heath conformed more closely to the popular concept of an artist. With his flashing eyes, slightly flamboyant manner and resplendent fame, he could hardly have failed to be a success with women. At the age of twenty he had married Eliza, the daughter of a Welsh clergyman named Thomas. Whether the life of the art-world in Georgian London proved too much for the daughter of the manse – and certainly her portrait suggests that the lovely Eliza was well aware of her attractions or whether George was responsible for the breakdown of the marriage, we do not know. But the fact remains that within five years of being married, and soon after the birth of their only son George, the pair separated.

Eliza, the first wife of James Heath. All the Heaths were notable for their choice of outstanding beauties

A later George Heath, Cuthbert's cousin, who assembled the *Records of the Heath Family* in 1913, firmly lays the blame on his great-uncle. 'Owing to his misconduct,' he writes of James,

> his wife left him when her son was two or three years old, and returned to her own family in Wales. She subsequently 'married' a Captain Wilson, and by him had at least two daughters.

What the Reverend Thomas thought of these goings-on is not recorded. Nor is there any mention of a later meeting between the separated pair. George, the child, remained with his father, who went to live with his housekeeper, a Mrs Philipson, by whom he had four more children. One of them must have been born around 1789, for in that year, we learn, James Heath lost a great deal of property, including etchings and engravings, in a fire –'and nearly lost his own life in rescuing his infant child.' He retired in 1822, lived his later years at Lewisham and died in 1834 at Coram Street.

Thus the Heath family had made their first outstanding contribution to the life of their times. Three of James's four children by Mrs Philipson also seem to have become artists, the best-known being Charles Heath, who was famous in his own time for the popular *Heath's Book of Beauty*.

The Heath family, legitimate or otherwise, were beginning to show striking talents. In the case of James' son George, however, these were to take a new direction.

There is nothing unusual in the reaction of children against their parents. We all know of radical children who rebel against conservative fathers, of artistic sons who are disinclined to follow in their father's more conventional footsteps. What is less commonplace is the reverse process – the reaction of a more sober-minded son against a free-and-easy parent. This was the story of George Heath's relations with his father.

Today a woman leaving her husband usually takes her children with her. But in those days the obloquy attaching to such an act was complete. Eliza, retreating to her native Wales and eventually to the arms of Captain Wilson, must have seemed no better than a fallen woman and certainly no proper parent. George remained with his father – though how he fared in the engraver's somewhat Bohemian household one can only guess. 'He cannot, I think, have derived much benefit from home discipline and associations,' was the dry comment of his own son Douglas, in a memoir written later.

There is no record of where George went to school, but we do know that at an early age, his father had him apprenticed to a fellow-engraver. But George was more interested in becoming a lawyer than in following his father's craft. In 1797 we find him in the office of a Mr Platt where he learnt not only law but ordinary academic subjects as well. By the time he was twenty-two, he noted in his commonplace book, he was reading Sallust at the rate of a hundred lines an evening. 'In French,' he continues, 'I am pretty perfect. I can read any book, and what is more, understand it, except technical words. I can read, without much difficulty, Italian novels and books.'

As to mathematics, he was in the middle of the sixth book of Euclid which he had gone through, he said, 'in a very slovenly manner, and dipped a little into Trigonometry ... My philosophical knowledge is merely superficial, having some ideas of Astronomy and read Chaptal, Lavoisier and Fourcroy on Chemistry.' When he came to the law, though, there was a note of ringing confidence. 'As to the law, that is my profession, and I cannot help continually improving.'

There is something about George Heath that makes him perhaps the most attractive of the Heath forebears. Comparing his portrait with his father's, one might conclude that here were James's dashing features grown, in the son, both more tender and more mature. 'I do not think he ever fell in with people whom he himself liked, without his becoming a favourite with them,' notes Douglas Heath,

Anne Raymond
Dunbar, wife of George
Heath. They bought
Kitlands, the first
Heath family home
in Surrey

who also records a touching story of how his father – who had
always cherished a romantic feeling for the mother he hardly knew
– once journeyed to Wales in the hope of seeing her. When he got
there she was away from home. He had to content himself, he said
sorrowfully, with seeing 'my two sisters over the garden wall.'

James Heath had put the family name on the map. But it was
George who became the founder of its fortunes. In 1806 – it was a
year before he was called to the Bar, but George always had a
cheerful way of being a little ahead of his expectations – he married
Anne Raymond Dunbar, the daughter of a Scottish lawyer.

That is perhaps to make the family sound too modest: the Dunbar pedigree was enough to make the Heaths look *arrivistes*. They could trace their ancestry back to Alfred the Great, and their territories back to the eleventh century when one Gospatric the Earl was given 'Dunbar, with the adjacent lands in Lothian' by King Malcolm Canmore. Since then eleven romantic generations of Dunbars had lived and died – often violently – in the misty lands around the Scottish borders. But not all Anne Heath's forebears were warlike. One, John Napier of Merchiston, was one of the great originators of mathematics who, in the seventeenth century, had invented logarithms – a genetic signpost, one might almost feel, to the inventor of non-marine insurance.

Meanwhile George Heath followed his call to the Bar in 1807 by a gradually increasing practice on the Home Circuit. Probably the increase was needed, for he was now the father of two children – Julia, born in 1807, and his eldest son John Moore Heath, born in 1808 and named after his godfather who was also his mother's cousin, Sir John Moore, the victor of Corunna.

But it was not only because of his growing family that George Heath tended often to be short of funds. All his life, according to the family records, he liked to live a little above his income and to 'be improving his dwelling or his estate, to have good furniture and good society, and to travel. Moreover he was prone to enter into speculation.'

Travel in particular was one of his passions. Evidently it was not shared by Anne Heath – who used to get annoyed by the habits of the French in whose company her husband took such delight. Perhaps that, as much as the fact that she was four months pregnant, was the reason that when he went to Paris during the summer vacation of 1810 he went without her – though armed with an introduction through his father to the Baron de Denon.

This remarkable character was then the director-general of museums. He had been a favourite both of Louis XV and of Napoleon to whom, during his campaigns, he had been adviser on which works of art were worth pillaging. He must have been impressed by the young English visitor who spoke such admirable French, for he gave him a suite in his house and introduced him everywhere – a compliment which George returned five months later when he asked him to be godfather to his second son, Douglas Denon.

The journal he kept of his month in Paris is a graphic record, packed with joyous and detailed accounts of everything from Versailles to the opera and the gambling-tables, from seeing Napoleon reviewing his troops to a new play at the Théâtre Française where he notes: 'The versification is evidently fluent and spirited ... I was

James Heath (1757–1834) was engraver to William IV

not a little pleased to find how well I could comprehend it.' It is the journal of a man of many-sided interests – and also, it is hard to resist the feeling, a little off the leash.

When he returned home it was with an unusual trophy – an Imperial Passport issued 'au Palais de Fontainebleau le 31st Octobre 1810' and signed by Napoleon himself. According to Douglas Heath's memoirs, 'the Emperor thought his ministers too lax in allowing passages to and fro into England, and had determined to sign all passports himself .... The story is illustrative of the way in which Napoleon meddled with the details of administration.'

In 1816 a chance came which seemed likely to resolve George's financial problems. He was offered the Chief Justiceship of New South Wales. After much deliberation he refused, on the ground that the money offered was not enough.

The decision seems to have been a turning-point. As if deciding that from now on he must make the best of things in England, he began to concentrate his mind more resolutely on his practice, beginning to specialize in insolvency and debt. Perhaps his own inclination to overspending gave him an insight into the debtors' problems. By 1819, at any rate, he was appointed Judge of a Small Debts Court.

Around this time he began to embark on a strenuous series of house-moves. Probably the motive was speculation rather than any kind of restlessness – he had burnt his fingers in the financial crash which followed the boom year of 1818, and perhaps he was trying to recoup the losses he had made then.

All the same the buying and selling of houses must have been exhausting for Anne Heath and the children – of whom there were now two more, Dunbar, born in 1816, and Leopold, in 1817. Between 1818 and 1825 he owned, at various times, five different homes. In 1818 the Heaths were living in Chancery Lane, the ground floor being George's chambers. There followed a move to Streatham, where he bought what would then have been a country house, with a good deal of land. Then, still keeping on the chambers, he took a house in Euston Square, sold the one at Streatham and in 1825 moved to Park Street, near Marble Arch. 'This last move,' thought Douglas Heath, 'was meant as a sort of compensation to my mother, to console her for the solitude and discomfort of Kitlands, which he had just bought and was gradually making habitable.'

It is the first mention of a house which was not quite to be dismissed along with Streatham and Euston Square. Whatever Anne Heath thought of the inconvenience of Kitlands, George Heath had found what were to become for all future generations of the Heath family their beloved acres.

George Heath (1779–1852) by Ramsay Richard Reinagle

The Imperial Passport, signed by Napoleon, on which George Heath travelled home from France in 1810

Leith Hill is today among the more familiar landmarks of the Home Counties, but neither the swirling traffic of the Dorking by-pass nor the picnickers on its still pine-clad slopes have yet spoilt it. Still crowned by the eccentric tower built in 1760 by a local land-owner who wanted to be buried there, it dominates the plain that stretches across the blue haze of the Weald as far as Chanctonbury Ring and the Sussex Downs.

When George Heath moved to Kitlands, Surrey seemed as remote from London as Cornwall or Northumberland. The surrounding countryside was wild indeed, compared to the more pastoral charms of Streatham, for highwaymen had frequented the district till as late as 1805.

Contemporary paintings of Kitlands show it as a somewhat ramshackle, simple farmhouse, but it must have seemed an enchanted haven after the family's recent wanderings. Lying on the east side of Leith Hill between the villages of Coldharbour and Holmwood, it looked over meadows and woods.

The Heaths must have decided to stay at Kitlands early on, for the move was followed by a process of gradual consolidation. In 1825 we read of a 'private road to Kitlands' being begun and a pond being finished. Five years later George notes the beginning of a drawing-room extension. Perhaps it was in the nature of a celebration, for in that year, 1830, he was granted the 'coif'– the wig of a Sergeant-at-Law.

Over the next few years he was gradually to extend the borders of his domain. Between 1830 and 1850 he bought two large neighbouring farms, Moorhurst and Trout's Farm, and a third, Anstie, which spread over the southern slopes of Leith Hill and included the site of an ancient British fortress. Between extending the estate, his work on the bench and his financial speculations, it must have been a hectic life. Later Douglas Heath wrote that he had a much more vivid recollection of the worry and miseries of that time than of his father's splendour.

One of the worries stemmed from his association with an American named Jacob Perkins, who had invented a means of engraving steel plates for the printing of banknotes so the notes could not be forged. Perkins' original idea had been to persuade the Bank of England to use his method, and one of his London contacts was Charles Heath, George's half-brother. Perkins' negotiations with the Bank of England were unsuccessful, but he did manage to get a contract with several of the other banks, who in those days could print their own notes. A company was set up with Perkins and the two Heath brothers as directors – George's shareholding being considerably the largest.

For a time the venture seemed one of George Heath's more promising speculations, but in 1826 a law was passed which forbade the private printing of notes worth less than £5. Charles Heath's finances could not withstand the blow. He went bankrupt, George taking on most of his debts. Eventually the company survived to repay George's efforts. Rowland Hill used the Perkins system for the production of the first Penny Postage stamp; the Queen's head was engraved by Charles in collaboration with Frederick Heath, presumably his brother.

Meanwhile there were family honours as well as problems. Both Douglas and his elder brother John were at Trinity College, Cambridge, and one can imagine the pleasure with which their father received, in January 1829, a letter from their tutor which congratulated him on

> the recent distinction gained by your sons, both of whom have passed most distinguished examinations . . . Douglas is very much the first man in his year. His abilities are of the very highest order, and I trust that he will aim at the very highest distinction which the university can offer.

Douglas was to prove his tutor's view well-founded. In 1832 he graduated as Senior Wrangler, adding for good measure a First in classics. Both he and John were members of Trinity's charmed circle, the Apostles. None but the intellectual élite of Trinity were invited to join the group, which gathered almost daily to discuss anything from politics to the Origin of Evil or the Derivations of Moral Sentiment. Among the Apostles was Alfred Tennyson, whose poetry was already being compared, at least by his contemporaries at Cambridge, to Milton's. His son Hallam Tennyson gives this picture of the Apostles in his biography of his father:

> There were regular meetings of the society as distinguished from the almost daily gatherings, at all of which much coffee was drunk, much tobacco smoked. The Apostle who proposed the subject for discussion, generally stood before the mantelpiece and said his say. Douglas Heath writes that the image he has carried away of my father is one "of sitting in front of the fire, smoking and meditating, and now and then mingling in the conversation . . ."

But it was not only his elder sons who were giving George Heath cause for pride. Leopold, the youngest, had already distinguished himself by winning the first medal at the Royal Naval College. In 1831, when he was still only fourteen, he was seeing service in a 74-gun ship in the Indian Ocean.

Meanwhile George's strenuous activities over twenty years were telling on his health. From 1837 onwards he began to suffer from nervous attacks in which, he said, his 'eyes were dazzled and he saw only half of any object he looked at.' Later he complained that 'he was unable to keep what he had to say well in his head.'

It was a sad decline for a man whose intellectual powers had been so forceful and wide-ranging, and George – fortunately no longer in debt or engaged in speculation – decided to retire from the law before his powers became weaker still. Four years later Anne Heath

The Penny Black, first
placed on sale on 1 May
1840. The central
feature of the design is
a portrait of Queen
Victoria aged eighteen,
engraved by Charles
and Frederick Heath
after a drawing by
Henry Corbould

died after a long and painful illness, and, sadly let off the leash this
time, he returned to his old love of travelling.

In its last decade his life seems to have had an Indian summer
quality. When Leopold was stationed at Malta, he would go there
with his daughter Emma: there were visits to Athens, where the
Sergeant's charm and style, and no doubt his copious store of anecdotes, made him a favourite with the British ambassador and the
other English residents. After Emma's marriage in 1845, he returned to Kitlands, still travelling to London and occasionally to
Paris. He died on 22 January 1852, 'surrounded,' said the *Law
Times*, 'by his friends after an illness of not long duration, in the
74th year of his age.'

Thus by the second half of the century the foundation of the dynasty was laid. James and George Heath, the founding fathers, were both dead. John Heath, the eldest of the new generation, was now vicar of Enfield. After leaving Trinity he had been called to the Bar but, according to an ominous note in the Heath records, 'the family affliction of deafness prevented his progress.'

Douglas Heath never quite fulfilled his early promise. Perhaps his talents, modesty, and easy good nature lacked direction. Apparently to please his father, he allowed himself to be steered towards the law, taking on a legal post originally meant for his elder brother. 'I was an unwilling victim at the time,' wrote Douglas later,

> wishing to stay at Cambridge and having no inclination to the life of a barrister. However, I cannot grumble now. I got the office, really that of a small debts court. On the establishment of county courts all over the kingdom, I was abolished, and appointed County Court judge for Bloomsbury.

Later in life he returned to his old love, mathematics – producing, in 1874, a book on the Conservation of Energy which was highly praised by Clerk Maxwell. For the rest he seems to have lived out his days as a benevolent squire and, as the family records put it, 'a superintending providence' to the village of Coldharbour.

No doubt it was a worthwhile life, but there was something missing – a sense of ambition, a certain thrust. Probably the point would later not be lost on Cuthbert.

All the Heaths typified their age. James Heath the engraver had been a true man of the Regency, while his son George had embodied the subtler qualities of the time when Georgian was shading to Victorian England, less profligate than its predecessor, more sensitive than what would follow. Even more than his father and grandfather, Leopold Heath personified the spirit of his age, the Victorian desire for solidity, combined with action and energy. His adventures must have seemed to his children like something from the *Boy's Own Paper*: as a young lieutenant during the capture of Borneo, he had led a party into the jungle to attempt the capture of a fugitive Sultan. In 1850 he had commanded a corvette engaged in the suppression of the slave trade off West Africa, and been the first man ashore in the attack on Lagos. Despite his bluff features and forthright manner he was a man of keen intelligence who, in the Borneo campaign, had taught himself enough Malay to act as a magistrate and interpreter in discussions with the Sultan.

On the outbreak of the Crimean War in September 1853 his corvette, the *Niger*, was ordered to the scene of hostilities. Leopold –

he had been promoted Commander six years earlier – was one of the beachmasters in the Crimea landing, and was later sent to take possession of the harbour at Balaclava. In October his ship took part in the bombardment of the Sebastopol forts, after which he was made battery officer under Sir Colin Campbell. In the December he took time off to return to Malta – one feels it was a snatched interlude in the smoke of battle – to get married.

Leopold was then thirty-six, and his bride was nine years younger. Her name was Mary Emma Marsh, and she came of the family who owned Marsh's, a private bank in Mayfair, which had a considerable naval connection and had been Nelson's bank.

Perhaps the link was a happy augury for a naval officer, for the next year, 1854, Leopold was promoted captain. His new command was the *Sanspareil*, a 74-gun battleship of the line, which took part in the second bombardment of Sebastopol in October.

Mary – such was the intrepid nature of naval wives – made several trips to Therapia in the Bosphorus to see him, otherwise staying at Malta where the Heaths' first child, Arthur, was born in October 1854. Following his birth she returned to England and began making a family home at Moorhurst, which had come to Leopold under his father's will.

LEFT Douglas Denon Heath

RIGHT Sir Leopold in old age

Meanwhile Leopold was given the key post of supervizing transport at Balaclava. 'I know no man so fit for it as you are,' wrote the Commander-in-Chief, Sir Edmund Lyons. Peace came to the Crimea in 1856, and he was given the command of coastguards between Dover and Southampton – partly to suppress the active smuggling trade along the south coast, but also to train the coastguards as a naval reserve.

The new command may have seemed unexciting after the almost continuous action he had seen since he was a boy. But it also meant a chance of family life with Mary and the two children he had hardly seen – Arthur, now two, and Marion, born the previous September at Moorhurst. Moreover his new command was based at Southampton, which is only sixty miles from Leith Hill. It would have seemed a long way in George Heath's time, but in 1858 the journey was startlingly reduced by the extension of the Woking-Guildford railway line to Haslemere and Portsmouth. If he needed to be at Southampton for any length of time, or if there was entertaining to be done, there were naval quarters for the family at Mersham, just outside Southampton: the Heaths' third child, Frederick, was born there in February. But whenever possible the family would hurry back to Moorhurst.

It must have been a golden time, that summer and autumn of 1858. There would be endless talk on a multiplicity of things with his brother Douglas just across the fields at Kitlands, and there would be fishing and shooting parties when the partridges and pheasant rose from the yellow broom that was Leith Hill's crowning glory.

Sometimes, too, he would stroll across the rest of his estates, for his father had left him not only Moorhurst but also 'Anstie Farm and the cottages and outhouses and lands adjoining'. Probably it was less imposing than it sounded – a mere clutch of buildings sprawled across the farmland on the south side of Leith Hill.

We have no record of when he first considered building a new house at Anstie. Perhaps he was beguiled by the view across the Weald, much finer than that from either Kitlands or Moorhurst, tucked away in the folds of the hill behind Coldharbour. He may have been looking for a use for the prize-money he had won after the Crimea. Perhaps above all he was the kind of man who, in the absence of Turks or slave-traders to be fought or Sultans to be captured, needed some kind of project.

Another consideration was that his family was growing larger. A fourth child would be born the following spring. His friend Sir William Eden had promised to stand godfather, and Sir William was one of the Lords of Admiralty.

If the child was a boy, he must have thought with satisfaction as he planned the possibilities of the new house, he would very likely join the Navy.

Cuthbert Heath was born, according to the notice in *The Times*, on 23 March 1859, 'at Forest Lodge, near Southampton, to the wife of Captain Heath, RNCB. Commanding HMS *Arrogant*.' The day seems to have been a wet and windy one, for several merchantmen outward bound from Southampton were forced to shelter in St Helen's Roads off the Isle of Wight because of the strong westerly winds.

Elsewhere the pages of *The Times* recorded the progress of a world between worlds. New attitudes and ideas were on the move, mingling with others that were dying. At Westminster, Parliament was discussing the perennial Reform Bill, while in America a sale of slaves was reported from Savannah. From Naples, Mr Reuter's new telegraph reported the arrival of the Grand Duke Constantine of Russia with an escort of four vessels. An advertisement announced a new popular work, Chambers' Encyclopaedia –'a dictionary of universal knowledge for the people'– to be published in weekly sheets priced at three-ha'pence. Other advertisements suggested a world poised between old technologies and new ones: cargo space was still available in 'the splendid clipper ship *John Bright*, famed for her rapid passages' to Sydney, while on a more modern note a neighbouring advertisement offered trips to Paris 'for 20s. or 28s. every Monday, Wednesday and Friday, by new and unrivalled fast steamships' from Southampton.

Once the child was safely delivered, Leopold Heath seems to have turned with relief to matters where he was more expert. The logistics of planning Anstie could have presented few problems to the man who had organized the transport at Balaclava, but they cannot have been easy. The name 'Anstie' comes from the Saxon 'ansteg', meaning a difficult place. In the mid-nineteenth century there was no access except by farm-tracks, and the site he had chosen was on a small ledge of the hill, a good five hundred feet up from Holmwood village. As to the design, the house would be of stone – handsome in the manner of its time, with high-pitched ceilings and tall windows to take in the sweeping views. But before the design could take shape, there was the immense labour of clearing the woodland site of the great trees which had grown there since Roman times.

It is not clear how long the building actually took, but Leopold himself notes that, after his coastguard command ended in 1861, he 'remained on half-pay, living at Moorhurst and superintending the building of Anstie Grange till 1862.' It is certain that the house was

Elephants are embarked aboard ship at Bombay. They were used as an unusual form of transport on the Abyssinian Expedition

completed by 1863, for in that year, he says, he was 'enabled to live at Anstie Grange' during his next appointment.

This was the vice-presidency of the Ordnance Select Committee which met three times a week at Woolwich. The duties seem hardly onerous, even by the standards of those days when it was possible to combine the roles of naval officer and country gentleman. But they were certainly useful – Leopold's own contribution was the introduction of the 18-ton 10-inch gun which was to remain for years the Navy's most formidable armament.

Meanwhile his seagoing days were by no means over. In June 1867 he was posted to Bombay as Commodore, second class, of the East India station. The posting led to one last adventure which was to be a worthy swansong.

Three years earlier, British public opinion had been outraged when King Theodore of Abyssinia had imprisoned Captain Cameron, the British Consul at Massawa. After interminable delays Mr Rassam, a former Assistant to the Political Resident at Aden, had been despatched to Theodore's court with a letter of protest from the Queen.

King Theodore's answer had been to put the envoy and the rest of his party in iron fetters. Across such distances, the news of this second outrage had only slowly filtered back to England. It was the summer of 1867 before – a little late but in true Palmerstonian style

The village of Akoo at
the head of Annesley
Bay. It was on this coast
that the final confron-
tation with King
Theodore took place

— a rescue operation was mounted, headed by General Sir Robert
Napier, Commander-in-Chief of the Indian Army based at Bombay.
Commodore Heath was given the task of ferrying a massive rescue
expedition to the port of Zoulla, on the coast of Annesley Bay on the
Red Sea.

Heath left Bombay just before Christmas in his flagship the
Octavia, with General Napier and his staff on board. The main body
of the expedition was carried in 669 troopships: it consisted of over
40,000 men, 22,000 assorted horses, mules and donkeys, 6,000 camels
and forty-four elephants.

The landing took place on 7 January. Leopold's role at Zoulla
apparently included the building of piers and stone houses – and
helping to solve the all-important problem of fresh water for the
troops. Eventually an answer was found by using the engines of the
troopships, some of which, he noted with modest satisfaction, 'were
fitted up with engines of a modern type, in which surface conden-
sation was adopted, and by a little ingenuity they were arranged so
as to give off fresh water of an excellent quality.'

The elephants played an unusual role in the action, according to
the stories with which Leopold, in later years, used to regale his
children. Brought from India to carry the guns over the mountains,
they terrified the Abyssinians, who had never before seen tame
elephants and thought they were some kind of magic beasts. Under-

standably giving up in the face of such numerous, large and magic foes, they drove their cattle towards the British in a traditional token of surrender. If the cattle were driven back, it was a sign that the offer of truce was rejected. If they were kept, it meant peace. The British, unfamiliar with such niceties of war, cheerfully kept the cattle and fought on.

Possibly helped by these unsporting tactics, the campaign was rapidly successful. The prisoners were released, following the battle of Arogyè in April 1868. King Theodore fought heroically, then killed himself in Roman fashion during the cannonade of the city of Mágdala on Easter Monday. In the honours awarded after the campaign, Leopold Heath was knighted, promoted to the command of the East India station, and had the pleasure of learning that both Houses of Parliament had voted that:

> the thanks of this House be given to Commodore Heath for the indefatigable zeal and great ability with which he conducted the naval operations connected with the transport of the troops and stores upon which the Expedition materially depended.

The tales of the campaign must have been spell-binding for the children. They were of an age to appreciate them – Arthur was thirteen, Marion twelve, Frederick ten and Cuthbert nine. By now he was no longer the youngest: Ada, later to be the closest to him, had been born in 1860, Herbert in 1861, and Gerard the youngest, in 1863.

No portrait exists of Cuthbert Heath as a small child. All we know of him is that he was quiet, good-natured, and noticeably taller than his brothers. His sister Ada later described him as a little withdrawn, partly because of a slight deafness which she thought attributable to adenoids. The earlier case of his eldest uncle John suggests an inherited family tendency as a likelier cause, but whatever the reason, his deafness seems to have become worse after an accident while his parents were stationed at Bombay. The young Heaths were being taken care of by an aunt, who wrote at the time about an accident while Bertie was boxing with his brothers. 'I believe,' she added, 'his deafness is worse since this happened.'

Even so it does not seem to have been much more than a mild inconvenience in childhood. Bertie, as he was known in the family, engaged in all the activities natural to the child of wealthy parents living in the country. He would go hunting or shooting with his brothers, riding over to Dorking, or sometimes for trips with his mother round the lanes in her little dog-cart. There were crab-apple fights in the glades, and mushrooming by moonlight, and at least once he had to be pulled out of the pond by his brother Freddie.

Sometimes there would be passing glimpses of a wider outside

BELOW King Theodore's Drinking Cup. It bears the inscription 'Taken by Lieutenant Kemp R.N. from King Theodore's house at the capture of Magdala 1868. Presented by him to Sir Leopold G. Heath, K.C.B., 1871'

OPPOSITE This family group was taken at Moorhurst in 1871. Cuthbert (*fourth from left*) is seen with his mother and brothers and sisters

A 'drawing-room' at
Buckingham Palace.
'Drawing-rooms' were
a feature of Queen
Victoria's court,
allowing her to favour
important subjects

world. On most days his uncle Douglas would stroll over from Kitlands, to talk to Sir Leopold about Garibaldi or to see his brother's
photographs of Abyssinia. There was at least one Sunday morning
family crisis when Sir Leopold walked out of Holmwood church
because he had been offended by the vicar's views on the Irish
question – not to mention the presence of candlesticks on the altar
which he regarded as a 'Popish gesture', according to Cuthbert's
daughter. After that the Heath family stopped going to Holmwood
church and went instead to Coldharbour, where the vicar was presumably less provocative.

But such hints of an outside world were peripheral to the
charmed circle of Anstie, Kitlands and Moorhurst. To the children
London must have seemed as remote as Abyssinia, or more so, for
they had seen their father's photographs of the campaign there.
Even so there were occasional reminders that London existed: in
the great cholera epidemic of 1866, which killed 6,000 people, mostly
in the East End, the Heath children were given beer to drink instead
of water, and fruit was, except for a modest ration of a dozen goose-
berries each, forbidden.

Education for Cuthbert's first eight years was in the schoolroom
at Anstie with a governess – or two, because the Heaths employed
both a French and German governess. (When the Franco-Prussian

war broke out in 1870, they had to be kept from meeting on the stairs, in case of altercations.)

At the age of eight, Cuthbert was sent away to prep school. The one chosen for the Heath boys – Arthur had gone the previous September – was Temple Grove School at East Sheen, which occupied the site of a former mansion which had stood between Mortlake and Richmond Park.

The headmaster and presiding genius of Temple Grove was an old Etonian and Fellow of King's College, Cambridge, named O. C. Waterfield, who had a considerable reputation as an educator in his time. In the view of A. C. Benson, a contemporary of the Heaths at Temple Grove and later Master of Magdalene College, Cambridge, Waterfield's strength lay in his ability to choose good staff and leave them to their teaching 'The comparative rarity of his appearances invested him with a mysterious awe,' wrote Benson.

> When he was arrayed in a full silk gown he was almost too majestic for words. A faint scent of Havana cigars hung about him. He walked with a slight limp, which gave him a swaying motion, and he had eyes of great brilliance which opened wide, if he was surprised or vexed, and struck terror into our souls. I have never in my life been so afraid of a human being as I was of him.

Temple Grove seems to have been conducted according to the theory that the less attractive the environment, the better the education. Classrooms and dormitories were bleak and barrack-like, and the diet was bleaker still: bread and butter and tea for breakfast, meat, pudding and beer for dinner, tea with bread and butter again at six o'clock and a simple supper at 8.30. According to his sister Ada, Arthur Heath always complained about the school food, and the standing joke among the boys was that Mr Waterfield kept guinea-pigs, which were served up to the boys for dinner.

Classics were pre-eminent in the curriculum at Temple Grove, with somewhat less attention paid to Divinity, Mathematics, German and French. Canings were frequent, but administered only by Waterfield himself. 'I still shudder at the sound of his bunch of keys, when he unlocked a drawer in his writing-table and pulled out a cane,' wrote Benson half a century later.

Meanwhile Sir Leopold's four-year posting to Bombay was drawing to a close. He returned to England in 1870 and was promoted to Rear-Admiral in the following year. Since 1869 he had also been a Naval ADC to the Queen, and on 28 March he and Lady Heath were summoned to a 'Drawing-Room' at Buckingham Palace. This was a kind of royal at home at which the Queen received not only her ministers, leaders of the armed forces and the entire diplomatic

RIGHT Brighton College
boys in 1886. They
travelled by stage-
coach for away
matches against
Lancing

OPPOSITE Masters at
Brighton College, 1871.
The Rev. John
Griffiths (*centre right*)
was headmaster in
Cuthbert Heath's time

corps but a list of other notables which filled three columns of *The
Times* Court Circular. The Queen, we read, wore a black silk dress
and the Order of the Garter, and was attended by the Prince and
Princess of Wales and the Princess Christian of Schleswig-Holstein.
It must have been a resplendent occasion, with half the élite of
England assembled in the full glory of that confident and vigorous
age. The Heath children were allowed a glimpse of their parents in
their finery. 'We all went up to London with Lizzy to see Papa and
Mamma dressed to go to the court to be presented to the Queen. It
was a very cold day,' noted Marion in the family diary.

Probably 'all' did not include the boys, for in September 1869
Cuthbert joined his brother Fred at Brighton College. The partings

Hounds meeting
outside Anstie Grange

at the beginning of term always cast a gloom at Anstie. 'I took
Fred and Bert to Brighton,' wrote Lady Heath. 'Very sad parting
with the dear boys.' There was sisterly as well as maternal sadness,
for Marion added: 'It is horribly dull for me for we have lost our two
Brighton boys.'

Brighton College was then, as now, perched high over the east
side of the town but in those days – it is a mile or more from the
Steyne – virtually in the country. Cuthbert himself later thought
that he had been sent to Brighton because it was supposed to be

good for his deafness. 'As a matter of fact, what with Brill's Baths and sea-bathing that was probably about the worst place I could have gone to.'

Even so it was a good setting for the son of a famous sailor, himself destined for the Navy, for there were then no blocks of flats or hotels to spoil the view from the flintstone buildings across the windy Channel. It must have seemed a long way from the comfort and closeness of the family circle at Anstie: school of any sort was a Spartan experience in those days. There were open fires in the classrooms but the general effect was of stone staircases and high-raftered rooms with gothic windows. As at Temple Grove, schoolwork hinged on the classics, but the only subject Cuthbert seems to have excelled in was French, for which he won a prize in the Christmas term of 1871. The book he chose for a prize, perhaps remembering his uncle Douglas's association with the poet, was Tennyson's *Idylls of the King.*

Not every end of term meant a return to Anstie. Following his promotion Sir Leopold had been put on to a committee to organize the defences against torpedoes in British ports. This involved longer – and from Lady Heath's point of view unwelcome – stays at Portsmouth. On 15 July 1871 she committed this *cri de coeur* to the family diary:

> We leave for that abominable Southsea on Monday next. Anstie looks reproachfully lovely – it is one of the few fine days we have had this summer. Goodbye my beloved Anstie for three months! May we all return in the same health and happiness as we leave it. Bert and Fred are to join us at 'Serpentine Road'!! ugh! from Brighton on the 27th.

The next few entries in the diary – it was written by various members of the family in turn – are worth quoting in detail, for they are the earliest surviving words of Cuthbert's.

> Saturday July 27th. Celebrate Ada's birthday. Fine in the morning – bathed, as we were dressing, it began to rain.

> Wet in the afternoon – read.

> Sunday 30th. Went to St Jude's church – tried to get a pew in the morning, but could not – so we had service at home. In afternoon went to church, found a pew, and stayed all the while, a collection at the end of the service (fine weather but windy).

> Monday 31st. Boys went boating in the morning. Arty and Mamma went to a ball on board the *Duke of Wellington.*

Were these golden days of childhood sometimes a little tinged with the perhaps uncomfortable knowledge that all Heaths were expected to follow the family tradition and make some major mark on the world? Sir Leopold certainly always expected his children to shine. Even the news that they were top of the class did not bring congratulation. Sir Leopold's somewhat gruff response was to ask why they were not bottom of the next one higher.

One other story of Cuthbert's youth may be significant. When he was very young he was mildly reproached by his mother because he had expressed an ambition to be rich one day. Perhaps the aspiration seemed a vulgar one in a family where material comfort was so much in evidence already, and perhaps too the remark stemmed from an instinctive feeling that his future lay in business and that because of his deafness he would never join the Navy.

Exactly when the blow – if indeed it was one – actually fell, we do not know. Cuthbert in an autobiographical note merely states that 'deafness early in life quite prevented' his godfather's nomination being used. In the normal course he would have gone to naval college at about the age of thirteen. So we can assume that in 1872 the decision was made that he should stay on at Brighton College. After that there seems to have been some discussion as to whether he might enter the Indian Civil Service, where Sir Leopold presumably had powerful contacts. But the project was 'abandoned for the same reason'.

Throughout his life Cuthbert Heath had one overwhelming asset. He knew how to capitalise his talents. It was to stand him in good stead in this first major crisis – and crisis it was, for everything must have seemed to suggest that whatever he did would be merely *faute de mieux*, a substitute forced on him by his disability. The one thing that had emerged from his schooldays was that he had inherited the family talent for languages. What he decided now was that this talent should be built on. At the age of sixteen he set off for France, spending six months with a family at Versailles and becoming 'quite proficient' in French. This stay was followed by another six months at Niort in the Deux Sèvres, between Poitiers and La Rochelle.

From France he went on to Germany, where – Cuthbert's original autobiographical notes are in the third person –

he studied the language at Bonn, becoming there a member of the University. After nine months employed in learning German, boating on the Rhine, and studying Chemistry in a very mild way ... an opening was found for him in Messrs Henry Head and Co.'s office, a firm of Lloyd's underwriters and insurance brokers.

Bearing in mind that it was written many years later, it is a sentence of quite startling modesty. It almost sounds like some slightly drifting relative being found a place for. Certainly it in no way

ABOVE The Tooley Street Fire in the summer of 1861 led to a growth in the demand for fire insurance

BELOW The Itaipu dam on the Parana river will produce the world's largest hydro-electric output. C. E. Heath has responsibility for the Paraguayan interests in this joint venture with Brazil. In 1978 a special ceremony to blow up the coffer dams and open up the diversionary channel was attended by the presidents of both countries

suggests the beginning of a career which was first to revolutionize
and then to dominate his chosen profession.

Perhaps indeed the realization of what he could achieve came
only gradually. When it did, it was the product of a flair whose
existence no one, including himself, had so far suspected.

Meanwhile there was one thing he had learnt from his childhood
that would never leave him. This was his sense of family solidarity
and loyalty which included the past as well as the present. Once,
many years later, he said a strange and revealing thing to his sister
Ada. 'I pray for us all every night, the living and the dead.'

ABOVE Lloyd's Under-
writing Room in the
1880s

OPPOSITE ABOVE The
south view at Kitlands
between the cedar and
tulip trees

OPPOSITE BELOW
Anstie Grange today.
The original house was
a good deal smaller

CHAPTER TWO

The Young Underwriter

ABOVE A glance at the Loss Book. The Loss Book is still an important feature of Lloyd's for it gives the first information that a ship has been lost at sea

PREVIOUS PAGE The reopening of the Royal Exchange, 28 October 1844. Besides the Queen and the Prince Consort, the roll call of celebrities present included Wellington, Peel and Gladstone

In early times the City had been the whole of London. Chaucer was born at Aldgate, and Thomas Becket within yards of where the Royal Exchange now stands. In 1597, among those recorded as not paying their rates in the parish of St Helen's, Bishopsgate, we find the name of William Shakespeare. Great merchants like Sir Thomas Gresham not only worked in the City but lived and died there – as their resplendent tombs in the City churches bear witness. The rich pattern of the City's social life in mediaeval times included Jews in Old Jewry and nuns, known as minoresses, in the Minories, where Cuthbert Heath House stands today.

Slowly over the centuries, London's centre of gravity shifted westwards, and the City became more and more exclusively dedicated to its ancient skills of commerce. When Cuthbert Heath came to Lloyd's, the City had not yet become a night-time desert, but the tendency was growing. New rows of villas were springing up in Kensington, Brompton and Hammersmith for the richer merchants, while their clerks moved out to Clapham, Islington and Peckham.

Cheapside, Poultry, Milk Street and Fish Street were becoming mere archaic names, their ancient trades forgotten as they were linked instead with vast new enterprises in banking, the money markets and insurance. Soon the City's dwindling resident population would decline further and more steeply. By the turn of the century, it would have become an enormous receptacle, an irregular square mile in size, into which thousands of people would be decanted to work each morning and poured back in the evening.

One of the decisive factors in these years of change was the coming of the railways. The new Liverpool Street Station had been built in 1874, bringing people from the new, fast-expanding suburbs almost to their office doorsteps. The streets themselves, though macadamised, were still gaslit, frequently foggy, and the unchallenged domain of horse-drawn carriages, slim and elegant hansoms, landaus, victorias and cabriolets.

There was a transformation in office building. The quarter's narrow streets became dominated by huge, ornate blocks, suitable repositories for the stores of wealth they symbolized. Grandeur, or grandiosity, was the order of the day: an architect would as soon have left off the roof of a new bank or insurance office as omit the

The Royal Exchange
in 1890

porticoes, stonc balconies or Corinthian columns. The same went
for their lavish interiors: the Anglo-Bengalee Disinterested Loan
and Life Assurance Company, which Dickens described with exul-
tant satire in *Martin Chuzzlewit,* must have been typical of many:

Within, the offices were newly plastered, newly painted, newly papered,
newly countered, newly floor-clothed, newly tabled, newly chaired,
newly fitted-up in every way, with goods that were substantial and
expensive, and designed (like the company) to last . . . . . . Solidity! Look
at the massive blocks of marble in the chimney-pieces, and the gorgeous
parapet on the top of the house! Publicity! Why, Anglo-Bengalee Disinterested Loan and Life Assurance Company is painted on the very
coal-scuttles. It is repeated at every turn until the eyes are dazzled with
it, and the head is giddy.

Dress reflected the general urge towards solidity and substance.
All City men – there were of course no girls – wore black, and the
more eminent would not be seen without a top hat and a sharp, un-
comfortably-edged wing collar. Beards, frowned on a few years
before, were almost universal among the upper classes by 1880. Quill

Royal Exchange
Buildings. It was here
that Cuthbert opened
an office in 1912

pens were still sold in the shops, and used in the more old-fashioned offices and certainly at Lloyd's.

The focal point of this swirling world of commerce was, as it still is today, a roughly triangular-shaped area bounded by the Royal Exchange, the Bank of England and the Mansion House. In earlier times this triangle had not existed. The old Royal Exchange had faced on to Cornhill, which then continued on to Poultry. The Mansion House had been built in 1724 on the site of an ancient market, while the open area to the west of the Royal Exchange had been the site of the National Lottery's office.

The Royal Exchange symbolized the continuity of the City as well as its substance. The first Royal Exchange had been opened by Queen Elizabeth in 1571. Its founder, Sir Thomas Gresham, had planned it on the pattern of the famous Bourse at Antwerp, as a sort of perambulatory meeting-place for merchants. Generations of bankers and merchants have trodden its famous – and still existing – floor of Turkish hone stone, for the character of 'Change, as it was known, was that merchants would walk while they struck their bargains. There were specific areas where one walked according to whether one wanted to discuss Greek, French, or Hamburg business. Great bankers like the Rothschilds and the Barings had fixed

positions beside the pillars, while there were 'firm oaken benches for the accommodation of those who were tired of pacing the ambulatories, and walls extensively illustrated with placards of ships about to sail; of goods to be sold; and lists of the sworn brokers of London.'

The Royal Exchange had also been the home of Lloyd's of London since 1773, when an underwriter named John Julius Angerstein had been seeking new premises for the writing of marine insurance. By chance he had heard of the availability of two rooms in the Royal Exchange 'late in lease to the British Herring Fishery', and acquired them. The result was that Lloyd's remained at the Royal Exchange till a cold and frosty night in 1838, when Gresham's historic building was destroyed by a fire, said to have begun at ten o'clock in the evening in one of the rooms used by Lloyd's underwriters. Whether the fire was in fact started by some roistering members of Lloyd's will, perhaps fortunately, never be known. Whatever its cause, the fire totally destroyed the building. Because of the ice on the roads, the horse-drawn fire-engines were slow in reaching the scene, and when they did, the water froze in mid-air as it rose from the hoses.

The new Royal Exchange building was opened with due ceremony

The Royal Exchange Fire, 1838. The firemen, according to a contemporary report, 'by a judicious but not very legitimate use of the engine hose kept the populace at a prudent distance.'

ABOVE Lloyd's sub-
scription room as it
appeared at the
entrance of Queen
Victoria

OPPOSITE The
commercial room at
Lloyd's from *The
Graphic*, 7 August 1886

by the young Queen Victoria six years later. The main event was an
enormous banquet, attended by the Queen, the Prince Consort,
Peel, Gladstone and the Duke of Wellington, who entered the re-
built Lloyd's Subscribers' Room to the strains of 'See the Conquer-
ing Hero'. Lloyd's underwriters, who had been temporarily and uncomfortably housed in South Sea House in Bishopsgate, returned
to their old home with relief. Since Cuthbert Heath was to work
there for nearly forty years, it is worth describing in a little detail.

If you approach the Royal Exchange from the east – by the broad
alley which today runs between Cornhill and Threadneedle Street –

you will notice on your right a small and unpretentious doorway. Once it had 'Lloyd's' written over the fanlight but the lettering has long since faded. Here the visitor would be greeted by a waiter in scarlet gown and tall silk hat and directed, according to *Punch* in 1880, up 'three flights of dark and dirty stairs fragrant with the fumes of smoke and cooking'.

This unpromising approach was evidently misleading, for on arrival in the Lloyd's Rooms upstairs the visitor was confronted with a scene of the utmost splendour. The rooms were, enthused the *Illustrated London News*, 'enriched after the best Roman models... Simple, massive, spacious and brilliantly lighted, they strike the

The Underwriting Room, Lloyd's. A Lloyd's man once said, 'Individually we are underwriters. Collectively we are Lloyd's', and it is in the Room that the individuals combine together to become the most important insurance market in the world

spectator at once with an idea of fitness – of adaptation to the exact wants of a great trading community.' The lavishness even extended to the toilets. 'The lavatory is on a scale approaching to luxury,' continued the report with reverence. 'The elegant soap-dishes, the spotless napkins, the china basins, the ivory-tipped cocks for the supply of hot and cold water . . .' But if the new Lloyd's Rooms were the preserve of a privileged élite, some were more élite than others. The poorer or less notable underwriters would sharpen their own quill pens, while the eminent had the sharpening done for them by the waiters.

Today the rooms are occupied, with an irony which the underwriters of the 1880s might have savoured, by the Guardian Royal Exchange Assurance Group, formed from a merger of two of their strongest competitors of those days. Despite recent modernization,

one can still see enough of the former outline of the rooms to sense their opulence: high fanlit windows, galleries, scrolls on the ceilings and huge palatial doorways.

Actual underwriting was done in the Subscribers' Room which occupied rather more than half the 11,000 square feet which Lloyd's rented for £1,200 a year. Here the underwriters sat, as they do at Lloyd's today, at small stalls or offices known as boxes. Basically a box consists of a table with a bench on either side: nowadays it may accommodate a dozen people, but in those days there would rarely be more than three or four. The other main point of difference from today was that each box had a high rail behind it, rather like a bedhead. At the sides of the boxes were large protruding wire baskets from which brokers would take their policies after signing. Gaslight bulbs hung in innumerable brass clusters from the ceiling. At

each end of the room there was an open fire at which 'underwriters would hitch up their coat-tails and warm their backsides'. Probably a more fresh-air-conscious generation would have sought to get away from the fire rather than near it, for the physical atmosphere of the Room was intolerably stuffy. 'You could cut it out and make boxes of it' was the reaction of one appalled North American broker, and even in the 1920s, Mr Bruce Miller recalls 'huge slabs of ice as big as tables' being brought in from Carlo Gatti's to cool the Room down.

Top hats were almost universal – one writer on Lloyd's attributed 'the prevalent baldness' of underwriters to the custom. On occasion they were put to somewhat rowdy uses, for Cuthbert Heath himself remembered that 'a certain underwriter who had endeavoured to divert business to himself by offering better commission had his hat smashed over his eyes.' But the most unfortunate of the physical hazards faced by underwriters seems to have been constipation. It is not clear whether this stemmed from the unhealthy atmosphere or the hardness of the seats, but one underwriter on the Heath box was ominously told by his doctor that he would never get rid of the ailment till he stopped working in the Room at Lloyd's.

At one end of the Room were the lists of shipping movements, while two huge ledgers, one recording safe arrivals and the other the sombre news of losses, were placed on high desks beside the entrance. Near the shipping lists was the rostrum from which the caller – in those days it was the famous Walter Farrant – would call the names of brokers. Farrant arrived at Lloyd's a little after Cuthbert Heath; till 1879, he had been a railway porter at Windsor station. It was here that his outstandingly clear and singsong voice had been noticed by a member of the Committee of Lloyd's while Farrant was calling train arrivals and departures.

Probably in those days there were not more than a hundred underwriters actively engaged in business in the Room. Even so, its hectic, crowded atmosphere impressed a reporter from *The Graphic* who noted that:

> The gangways between the rows of desks are thronged with brokers and clerks, with cases of 'slips' in their hands, passing to and fro between one underwriter and another. . . . No little dexterity is needed to avoid cannons and collisions as one pilots one's way along.

Underwriting hours – if one can go by Dickens' Mr Podsnap, who 'had thriven exceedingly in the Marine Insurance way'– were not vastly different from today. According to Podsnap, 'the world got up at eight, shaved close at a quarter-past, breakfasted at nine, went to the City at ten, came home at half-past five, and dined at seven.'

OPPOSITE The Loss Book. Shipping casualties are still recorded in the same way at Lloyd's today, written with the quill pen

BELOW Walter Farrant, the Caller. The Caller today still calls out from his rostrum the name of any broking firm and broker for whom he has information

Eating, then as now, was taken seriously in the City. All the great mercantile coffee-houses were gone by the 1870s, but chophouses like the George and Vulture and the famous Albion in Aldersgate Street still flourished. According to the London historians James and Muirhead Bone, one dinner given by a gourmet Victorian alderman cost about £30 a head at the Albion. Other chophouses catered for less well-lined pockets:

> Behind high backed and hard benched seats solid meals were served by waiters familiar to and with their customers. When the young man of the normal 9d. or 1/– lunch made a splash with his cronies they proceeded to one of the larger chophouses, selected with an air of wisdom their chop or steak and watched it being grilled to their direction. That was life! Then back to the cheap dishes in quieter places until pockets were replenished.

Just across the street from the Royal Exchange was Birch's confectioner's shop, famous for its orange jellies and three-decker sandwiches, said to have been highly favoured by Lloyd's underwriters. In his later years, Cuthbert Heath would often have a tray of lunch brought in from Simpsons in Cornhill, usually accompanied by a

Birch's confectioner's shop around the turn of the century

bottle of claret. Sometimes he was so busy that he forgot to eat it. If so, it would be gratefully disposed of by one of the junior clerks.

Meanwhile there were few eating-places in the City where the underwriters could get a better lunch, or perhaps simply a dozen Whitstable natives washed down with Chablis, than in the Captains' Room at Lloyd's itself. The name stemmed from the days of the original coffee-house, where a room had always been set aside for ships' captains who came to discuss their insurances, or to buy a ship at auction. In the 1880s, seafaring men were a common sight at Lloyd's: one of the most charming evocations of those days – still preserved in one of the executive corridors of the offices of the Guardian Royal Exchange – is a small recessed seat, appropriately rather like an upturned boat, where a captain might sit while waiting at the entrance to the Subscribers' Room to see an underwriter. Even in the bustle of a modern insurance office it is not hard to imagine some seafaring character sitting there, bringing a tang of the sea to the historic market.

Such a figure would also have been a symbol. Lloyd's in the 1880s was almost exclusively a marine market, and the reputation of a captain was the best guide for an insurer. But failing a personal

The telegram room in the Royal Exchange, 1886

acquaintance, an underwriter would look up a captain's record in the Captains' Register. Cuthbert Heath, in his early days as a marine underwriter, used it often. 'I can well call to mind the careful scrutiny of the Captains' Register', he recorded in a memoir. 'When so much depended on seamanship, the record of the Captain largely influenced the acceptance or otherwise of a risk – more especially as regarded sailing-ships.'

It was a far cry from the kind of risks he was to write later. Meanwhile how had the name of a seventeenth-century coffee-house proprietor come to be equated with marine insurance?

On 7 December 1601 the first Bill relating to insurance was introduced to Parliament by Francis Bacon. Headed 'An Act touching policies of Assurances used among Merchants', it stated that in such an assurance: 'it comethe to passe, upon the losse or perishinge of any Shippe there followethe not the undoinge of any Man, but the losse lighethe rather easilie upon many, than heavilie upon few.' Specifically, it is worth noting, the majestic phrase related to marine insurance. Not for another sixty years, at least until after the Fire of London, would people even begin to think in terms of insuring other kinds of property than ships or cargoes.

In early times the London insurance market had been centred on Lombard Street, so named by the Italian merchants who seem to have brought their underwriting skills to London before the end of the fifteenth century. By 1576, according to Harold Raynes, the market 'had gravitated to the Royal Exchange from Lombard Street.' Within less than a century it had moved again, this time to a coffee-house in Tower Street.

The new custom of doing business in coffee-houses had boomed ever since a Ragusa merchant named Pasqua Rosee had opened the first coffee-house in Cornhill in 1652. Half a century later there were said to be 3,000 such establishments in London, mostly with a specialist clientele of their own. For the poets and wits there was Will's in Covent Garden. The doctors' haunt was Child's, in St Paul's Churchyard, while the City had its own thriving network in the narrow courts and alleys round the Royal Exchange. Garraway's and Jonathan's were the most famous of them, but for those connected with marine insurance there was one coffee-house that mattered – the one kept by Mr Edward Lloyd in Tower Street. There is no record of when it opened, but we do know that by 1689 it was regarded as the main source of information for the marine insurer not to mention ships' masters and their owners.

By the turn of the century ship sales were being held at Lloyd's coffee-house, and the coffee-house had its own news-sheet, *Lloyd's*

News, which gave daily information on shipping movements. If an important announcement was to be made – it might be bad or good news, a loss or the arrival of an overdue ship – it would be announced in ringing tones by one of the coffee-house waiters known, for reasons which have not come down to us, as the Kidney.

Later these homely arrangements would become more formal, largely as a result of the reforms, brought in by Angerstein, which transformed Lloyd's from a coffee-house run by its proprietor to a market run by the underwriters. Nevertheless the tradition of the early days still lingered on. The red-robed waiters who greeted Cuthbert Heath in the Room in 1877 were called waiters rather than servants or commissionaires because the basic pattern was still that of Edward Lloyd's time. The place where an underwriter wrote his risks was called a box and not a desk because it, too, followed the division of the coffee-house into pews or benches.

There was another still more significant way in which the Lloyd's of the 1870s resembled the coffee-house. The seventeenth-century underwriter had been an individual. In those early days there were no such things as insurance companies – if a ship he had insured went down, he and the rest of those who had signed the slip must pay up their own money. Later the capacity – the amount of insurance he could write – would be increased by the formation of what were known as syndicates, composed of what were later to become

Lloyd's Coffee House, 1740. Edward Lloyd provided his customers not only with pen and ink but also with details about ships' arrivals at the wharves, casualties and later about ships for sale

Lloyd's Rooms, 1809

known as underwriting 'names'. Many of the names were simply wealthy individuals who had pledged their names and fortunes to the underwriter who wrote for the syndicate. If a ship they insured went down, they would have to pay their proportion of the loss. If it did not, they would receive their share of the profit.

Such were the means by which the market worked. But how profitable was it in practice? The answer must be that it was not – or at least, not nearly as profitable as it should have been. For half a century before the arrival of Cuthbert Heath, Lloyd's had suffered a sad decline, both of its business and its reputation.

Partly the reasons were historical. Lloyd's traditional marine dominance had, in the past, been greatly helped by an Act of Parliament of 1720. This stated that marine insurance could only be written by individual underwriters – in other words Lloyd's – and two licensed companies, the Royal Exchange and London Assurance corporations. Neither company had taken great advantage of the

monopoly, for both were primarily fire insurers. As late as 1810, Lloyd's was virtually the London marine insurance market.

Then in 1824 a hammer-blow had fallen. The century-old monopoly had been repealed, releasing a flood of new companies onto the London market. Many were short-lived: the year 1839 alone saw the formation of seven marine companies, only one of which survived till 1860. Even so these mushroom companies left their mark, for nothing is so bad for the insurance business as a proliferation of new and unskilled underwriters who tend to quote unrealistic rates, thus dragging the market down with them.

There were other and more serious rivals. In 1863, three new companies, the British and Foreign, the Commercial Union and Union Marine, all started writing marine business. Soon they were beginning to outdistance Lloyd's.

But its competitors were not Lloyd's only problem. The fact was that it had lost its zest for pioneering. From the 1860s onwards the market was virtually paralysed by a malaise, a lack of the enterprise and response to new demands which is the essence of insurance. One visible sign of this was the lack of young men at Lloyd's – the promising younger ones had all been snapped up by the companies. Significantly, one of the first things Cuthbert Heath noticed when he came to Lloyd's was how old the underwriters were. 'Age generally brings caution with it and people were more conservative, often an underwriter would ask for a day or two to think over a risk . . . One remembers the care with which the twenty or so risks,

An underwriter, by a *Graphic* artist in 1886. The name 'underwriter' is derived from the practice of men writing their names one under the other to cover an insurance risk which then meant a decent day's work, were watched.'

The market was not only cautious – always a cardinal sin in Cuthbert Heath's book – but unadventurous almost to the point of inertia. There were many outside who thought it likely to become a merely quaint survival. 'The Committee walks in shackles and mistakes its awkwardness for dignity,' wrote J. T. Danson, a Liverpool company underwriter who delivered a series of ferocious salvoes on Lloyd's in the 1870s. 'The ease of routine and the dignity of prestige – the natural consolations of respectable senility – have long superseded the elasticity of youth.'

True, Danson had an axe to grind. His aim was to secure representation of the companies on the Committee, thus gaining access for them to its information services on shipping movements. But even Charles Wright and Ernest Fayle, the historians of Lloyd's, concede that there was a 'sub-stratum of truth' in Danson's attack. Lloyd's had lost its traditional confidence and sense of panache. Premium income was falling everywhere. What business there was, was not shown first to Lloyd's. By the 1870s it had become, Wright and Fayle admit, 'scarcely more than a supplementary market'.

'Cuthbert is now eighteen,' wrote his mother in the spring of 1877. 'He was recalled last winter to take a place as junior clerk in Messrs Head's office at Lloyd's – where Bertie is working now – coming to us every Sat. and Sunday.'

The Messrs Head referred to were insurance brokers and underwriting agents. Beside the insurance side of their business, they also had considerable interests in several of the north-eastern shipping firms for whom they were insurance brokers.

Heads had been founded in 1860 by Henry Head, one of a Quaker family from Ipswich. Though he had by then left the Society of Friends he remained, we read, 'a strong evangelical Christian, imbued with the Quaker belief that a business diligently and honestly conducted, could be carried on to the glory of God.'

Such a statement may savour a little of smugness today, but it is worth noting that Cuthbert, who was deeply religious throughout his life, should have come into contact with so strong and serious a view of business ethics. The life of the City was to be greatly enriched in the later years of the century by a new strain of zealous, often strict-living Nonconformists who would bring new standards of probity to business. Stemming as it did largely from the middle class, the Nonconformist view was perhaps at variance with his own more patrician background. Even so it was to show itself in the trust he later placed in such men as Arthur Burns and H. S. Spain, both ardent Nonconformists.

ABOVE 'Path to the High Field' by Cuthbert Heath. The dedication to Sarah is just visible in the top right-hand corner

BELOW 'Niort' by Cuthbert Heath. Cuthbert always took his painting materials when travelling abroad

The path to the thyrs Field
Anstie (Given to S.G.G.)
1882 View from Lower Garden

Niort 1878

According to one story, Cuthbert's first job at Heads was filling up the inkwells: most likely it is true, for he himself later recalled that he began 'at the very bottom of the office'. He does not tell us what he earned, but Heads seem to have been more generous than most City firms: Charles Wright, who joined them shortly after Cuthbert, recalled receiving £100 a year as a starting salary – a large sum for a young man in those days.

Meanwhile in the wider world of Lloyd's there were the first movements of a new mood stirring. Cuthbert's arrival, as we saw, had coincided with the worst times for Lloyd's underwriters that any could remember. The market was still far from meeting the challenge from the companies, but at least there were signs that the old initiative glimmered.

One reason for increasing confidence was that in 1874 the Committee of Lloyd's had made one of its more fortunate appointments. It had chosen as Secretary a former army officer, then in his thirties, named Henry Hozier. By the 1880s he was already making his mark at Lloyd's with a new scheme whereby cargo claims could be paid in foreign ports. Eventually the scheme brought a large volume of business back to Lloyd's, while later still Hozier's name was to gain an enduring fame when his daughter Clementine married a rising young Liberal politician named Winston Churchill.

Another Lloyd's figure of the time was a marine underwriter named Frederick Marten. Cuthbert must have known him well, for the two men's boxes adjoined each other in the market. It was an odd coincidence, for Marten was himself a notable innovator.

Marten deserves a place in any history of Lloyd's because it was he who invented the concept of large syndicates. The point is specially relevant for us because it was one that Cuthbert himself was to grasp at eagerly a few years later.

No insurance undertaking can prosper unless it is backed by capacity – the financial resources to back the large spread of risks a successful underwriter needs to have. Lack of capacity had been one reason why, in the mid-seventies, Lloyd's had lost out to the companies. The individual syndicates were simply too small to take the risks on offer. At that time it was exceptional for a Lloyd's syndicate to include as many as six people. The majority were composed of two or three, while one in five consisted only of a single individual.

At a time of rapidly increasing values, capacity on this scale was derisory – but it took the insight of Frederick Marten to see that the days of small syndicates were over. Soon he was writing for a syndicate of twelve names. His lines – or shares of a risk – were large enough to make the more conventional Lloyd's men gasp. The

ABOVE The view from Villa Savaric at Eze. Cuthbert was still painting water-colours in his seventies

BELOW 'Cuthbert Heath' by Sir William Orpen, R.A. This was the picture presented to him by his syndicate in 1921 and the original now hangs in C. E. Heath & Co's boardroom

Room hummed with prophecies that he was riding for a fall, but Marten remained firmly in the saddle. By the 1880s the volume of business on his syndicate exceeded even that of the large companies.

While Marten was thus gradually pulling the marine business back to Lloyd's, Cuthbert Heath was placing his first steps firmly on the ladder – though 'not making a fortune yet', his mother confided to her diary. In 1880, having reached the minimum age of twenty-one, he became an underwriting member of Lloyd's. Helped by a loan of £7,000 from his father, he joined the syndicate of J. S. Burrows. 'The connection,' he later wrote, 'was not a very successful one and I can well remember being aware of the vicissitudes of things by six or seven small grain vessels on which we had lines, being wrecked by one gale in the North Sea.' By the next year he had begun underwriting for himself with a syndicate of three names. In January 1883 his business had grown large enough for him to employ a clerk, and in the same year, his mother noted, he began a brokerage business – 'his dear father,' she added happily, 'having as usual exerted himself to get Bertie brokerage and succeeded.'

In one sense, it must be said, Cuthbert was fortunate. His father was able to help him financially, and he was saved the slow and weary effort of having to push his way up from nothing. But this superficial advantage was more than balanced by a darker aspect – the sense that he had been provided for and set up to earn a safe, prestigious, but relatively unexciting living as an underwriter.

Did he sometimes overhear, despite his deafness, the family saying that 'poor Bertie had to go into the City'? Earlier we noticed that 'he was found a place for' at Heads and his mother's diary says he was 'recalled' from the Continent to begin work there. Many years later, according to one newspaper obituary, he told his friend Sir Edward Mountain that he had in his youth been regarded as 'the fool of his family'. The words may been spoken lightly, but they must have bitten deep to be so long remembered. Probably his family's attitude was on the whole meant kindly: the City was a convenient second-best, a place of respectable, rather orthodox dullness where no one was expected to shine – indeed where brilliance might seem a disadvantage. Because of his deafness, one almost feels, he was excused the obligation of adding to the family roll of honour.

Was it his reaction to his family's attitude that gave him his edge of resolution? If so it was new-found, for it had not been apparent in his schooldays. What does seem clear is that at some point in those early years at Lloyd's a new sense of purpose, perhaps unconsciously, stirred in him. Like Philoctetes in the legend, he would transform his wound into a bow.

Somewhere, in the apparently unpromising context of insurance, he would find and mark out a territory of his own. The territory, when he found it, was to be the new world of non-marine insurance.

It is in some ways astonishing that Lloyd's, during its long pre eminence in marine insurance, had never seriously considered the possibility of writing what are known as non-marine risks – that is, anything other than ships or ships' cargoes. It is true that around the end of the eighteenth century a few underwriters wrote a certain amount of fire insurance until, for taxation reasons, the business ceased to be profitable. But by and large the tradition was that the companies wrote fire risks and Lloyd's marine risks with – until the removal of the monopoly in 1824 – little or no overlapping.

Around 1870 the concept of a small fire market at Lloyd's had been revived. Perhaps it originated partly as a consequence of the companies' growing encroachment on Lloyd's ancient marine pre-serves, but a stronger reason was that the huge spread of trade meant that industrial fire risks were growing larger. Warehouse fires in particular caused damage that was, by the standards of the time, catastrophic. In 1861 the Tooley Street fire in Bermondsey

Fire engines go to a fire in central London. Non-marine insurance before the days of Cuthbert Heath was largely the province of the insurance companies

A fire in Clerkenwell, 1885. It was about this time that Cuthbert Heath became involved in non-marine insurance

was said to have lighted London at night 'as though by a huge torch' and cost the insurance industry upwards of £21 million.

There is no indication of how large the Lloyd's fire market was, or of how many underwriters specialized in the business. What is certainly true is that they saw it as a sideline to their ordinary marine underwriting. Most likely it would have continued as one had Cuthbert Heath not been seeking a new field to conquer.

Probably he was not consciously thinking of non-marine insurance as his chosen territory, but lucky chances usually come to those prepared to use them. His lucky chance came in 1885 through his father who happened to be a director of a fire insurance company called the Hand-in-Hand. Dating back to 1696, the Hand-in-Hand was one of the oldest insurance companies in the country. Partly because of its ancient origins it was listed as a mutual. This, in insurance terms, means a group of people, usually in the same line of business, who come together to pool premiums, thus paying for each other's potential losses.

Now, in 1885, the Hand-in-Hand was seeking a reinsurance

treaty – the method by which an insurer seeks to unload a proportion of his own risk onto others. But under insurance law, a mutual
was not allowed to reinsure with tariff companies. Not unnaturally,
Admiral Heath had thought of Lloyd's and more especially of
Cuthbert. No Lloyd's underwriter had ever previously considered
writing reinsurance on fire business – not because there was anything particularly hazardous about it, but simply because it had
not been the custom at Lloyd's to write that type of business.

The twenty-six-year-old Cuthbert Heath's acceptance of the
Hand-in-Hand reinsurance is a milestone not because of the nature
of the risk itself, but because of the manner of his acceptance. True,
he was in one sense helped once more by his father. But he was
helped far more by what was now strongly emerging as his own
underwriting temperament – a freshness of approach which saw no
reason not to do a thing simply because it had never been done
before. In the words of D. E. W. Gibb:

> Heath found the novelty an attraction, not a deterrent. If there was a
> reason to prevent him from writing the risk it must lie in the quality of
> the risk itself. If the risk was a bad one, then either the rate must be
> raised to an appropriate level, or it must be turned down. But a risk that
> had nothing against it except its novelty was the best of all risks to write,
> for the underwriter who accepted it would be starting on the ground
> floor and establishing himself as a market before his competitors.

What Cuthbert Heath had achieved, and got away with, was the
formulation of a heresy. He had dared to deny that the business of
Lloyd's was above all to write marine risks.

It was the first step, but it was as nothing to what would follow.

CHAPTER THREE

The World at Risk

Historians often make the point that when an ailing regime is about to be replaced, the moment of change does not come when things have reached rock-bottom. The truly significant change usually comes later, when they have begun to improve a little.

This was precisely the pattern of events at Lloyd's during the 1880s. Following the intense competition from the companies, Lloyd's had lost not only premiums but its sense of purpose. Then had come a breathing-space while Frederick Marten's innovations had helped the market to set its house in order.

But Marten was still only concerned with the marine market. Nobody at Lloyd's except Cuthbert Heath had grasped the simple point that there was no reason on earth why it should not enter the new and potentially vast field of non-marine insurance. At first he was met with the usual derision that greets the pioneer. Following his reinsurance of the Hand-in-Hand, we read, 'the general attitude towards his enterprise was such that there was betting on how long it would be before he was ruined.'

Cuthbert himself seems to have reacted with characteristically cool good humour. His proposals, he wrote later:

> were considered as radical innovations which should not be considered seriously. Other members, one by one, however, began to show an interest in the business. In those days the market, which consisted of the fire companies only, was not big enough for all the larger risks which had to be covered, and the opening of Lloyd's to this business filled a long-felt want.

The words are a modest summary of a period of prodigious change. But what was it about Cuthbert Heath that enabled him, at twenty-six, to begin steering the historic market in a totally new direction? If we look at the photographs of him taken at the time, we see a young man already confident. Partly, no doubt, the confidence stemmed from his background, for people with a family tradition like the Heaths tend to be that much more adventurous, that much less conforming.

But above all one senses the exhilaration of a young man who has found his *métier*. It is the romance of Lloyd's that a man sits at a tiny box – itself not unlike a life-raft adrift on some perilous sea –

PREVIOUS PAGE
Dickins & Jones, the department store, in Regent Street. Growing Victorian affluence encouraged the development of non-marine insurance

and there proceeds to put his name to a piece of paper which may ruin him or make his fortune. Add to this the fact that Cuthbert was young, ambitious and doing something no underwriter had done before him. From the start his underwriting was positive, aggressive and – perhaps the most important point – a pleasure. 'He never seemed to seek a reason for declining a risk,' said one man who, many years later, sat at the box beside him. 'He always looked round for a reason and a basis whereby he could write it.'

Even so the new age of Lloyd's was only just beginning. Until now Cuthbert had written risks which were new to the market, but not to the industry in general. The next step he took was to be far more outrageous.

He always saw the role of insurance as being to serve the needs of industry in general. Now, at this early stage in his career, he was aware of an outstanding gap in the cover that insurance offered. The gap lay in the fact that if a businessman had his premises destroyed by fire, he would face the problem of a loss of profits. It might be six months or a year before he could rebuild his premises and get production going again, and during that time his business would be earning nothing. Then why not devise a policy which would cover the businessman for this loss – calculating the payment made as a percentage of the amount paid out on his actual fire insurance?

Insurance companies do not always take the most generous view

London Bridge Station. The development of transport to the suburbs meant that the city declined as a residential area

of human nature, and no sooner had Cuthbert started writing the new policies than there came a storm of protest. He was summoned before the chairman of the Fire Offices Committee and told that he was 'ruining fire insurance'. The new policy, the companies said, was an open invitation to the public to defraud insurers. How would an insurance company be able to know that a businessman's estimate of his loss of profits was correct? What if he cooked his

LLOYD'S BURGLARY THEFT & FIRE POLICY.

In the name of God, Amen. Whereas

£ 200

No. 60845

E F A Green has paid £ Premium or Consideration to Us, who have hereunto subscribed our Names to Insure *him* from Loss by Burglary Theft or Robbery with or without violence, or by Fire, of the property herein specified, or any part thereof, from or at the premises herein mentioned, during the period from the

18th day of July 1904 to the

17th day of July 1905 both inclusive

and 15 days' grace for renewal.

Property Insured.

£ 200 on the whole Contents of *14 Alexandra Road South Woodford*

in the occupation of the Assured.

Including risk of damage done by Burglars.

Now know Ye, that we the Insurers do hereby bind Ourselves, each of his own Part, and not One for Another, our Heirs, Executors, and Administrators, to make good to the said *E F A Green* his Executors, Administrators, and Assigns all such Losses, not exceeding the Sum of *Two hundred pounds* in all as he or they may from time to time sustain by any such Theft or Robbery or Fire as aforesaid during the said period, within Thirty Days, after such Loss is proved, and that in proportion to the several Sums by each of Us subscribed against our respective Names.

Provided always that there shall be no Claim on this Policy when the whole loss by theft or robbery on any one occasion does not amount to £5; or for loss by theft, robbery, or misappropriation by members of the Assured's household, business staff, or other inmates of the Insured premises.

No claim to attach to this Policy for loss resulting from Insurrection, Riots, Civil Commotion, or Military or Usurped Power.

~~Subject to the Conditions of Average~~ (See Paragraph No. 1 on next page) *aly*

This insurance is subject to the conditions endorsed hereon, but in the event of loss by Fire the £5 Clause and Average Clause do not apply.

IN WITNESS whereof We have subscribed our Names and Sums of Money by us Insured.

Dated in London, the 15th Day of July One Thousand Nine Hundred and four

£1 (one pound) aly

C. E. Heath
J. S. Follett
F. Heath
G. Heath
A. D. Whitman
S. S. Weatherley

EACH ONE SIXTH

£ 200

of Two hundred pounds
for W A F Pryce

books to make a claim? Or even resorted to arson if his business was doing badly?

We have no record of what Cuthbert told the chairman of the Fire Offices Committee. Probably he listened with his customary courtesy. Certainly he went back and continued, undeterred, to write the business. No more seems to have been heard from the companies – except that, before long, they were paying him the compliment of imitation. As a result, says Gibb:

> there is probably not one fire office in the country that refuses to give cover for loss of profits: not one that does not value a branch of its business which Heath's enterprise forced them to start so reluctantly.

Meanwhile his own underwriting was rapidly expanding. 'Cuthbert working well at all his business of brokerage and insurance and getting well off, I hope,' noted his mother in her diary in April 1887. Her hopes were justified. In the same year he began writing specifically non-marine business for a syndicate of fifteen names. The lesson of Marten's larger syndicate was well taken.

In that same year another innovation was to follow. It was the most far-reaching yet, for till now Cuthbert had dealt only in the kind of risks that would be of interest to businessmen and to other people in insurance. The fact that something new was happening at Lloyd's had not yet filtered through to the general public, who still thought of Lloyd's as an historic, somewhat picturesque, institution to do with marine insurance.

Cuthbert Heath's next move was to bring Lloyd's a good deal closer to the man in the street.

Burglary was the terror of the middle classes in the '70s and '80s. Their favourite bogeyman was the notorious Charles Peace, a Yorkshireman who had fled south after murdering his mistress's husband in Sheffield. For two years he had remained in hiding in South London, committing scores of burglaries till he was finally caught at Blackheath. The unsuitably-named Peace had been hanged in 1879, but his fame was such that he bred a host of imitators, and between 1885 and 1888 the number of burglaries in the London area nearly doubled. Yet, remarkably, there was no such thing as burglary insurance.

The story of how it began is one of the classics of insurance history. One day a broker was at the Heath box renewing a fire insurance. Half-jokingly, he asked if the syndicate would also quote a rate to cover the house in question against being burgled. Cuthbert Heath considered for a moment, then said two simple words – 'Why not?'

Cuthbert Heath's 'Why not?' has become legendary not only because it began a new epoch in insurance. The phrase also summed up his view of underwriting. No matter how unconventional a risk might be, it should be considered on its merits. An underwriter was there to write the business offered, not to decline it.

It took a little time before the public learnt that, as ordinary householders, the resources of the Lloyd's market could now cover them against the risk of burglary. The Heath policies were first revealed in a popular monthly, the *Oracle*, in October, 1889. A few days later the story was picked up by the widely-read *Pall Mall Gazette*. The basis of the report was an interview with the

Charles Peace

broker who had placed the first insurance. His name was W. H. Wood and his firm, Pickford Bros., of 36 Cornhill, had issued a circular saying they 'were prepared to effect insurance at Lloyd's against the risks of loss by theft or robbery, with or without violence, or burglary.'

The report was also illuminating as to detail. Two shillings and sixpence per cent was the premium for the contents of a whole house: this was increased to three and fourpence if the assured householder wanted to include damage done or caused by burglars. The same rate obtained where specially selected articles, such as plate and jewellery, were to be insured, but this premium dropped to two and sixpence if the selected articles were normally stored in a safe. On business premises there was a special rate: five shillings was the normal premium, or three and fourpence if 'special precautions were taken to protect the property'. Claims would be paid within thirty days after a loss. 'Mr Wood further informed our representative that several losses have already been made good – notably, one quite recently at Harringay, for £25,' concluded the report in the *Pall Mall Gazette*.

The *Oracle* went into far more probing detail. Would not burglary insurance, its reporter asked, offer a premium to carelessness on the part of householders? Mr Wood's answer was interesting enough to be worth quoting in detail:

> That was a point which was disposed of when fire insurance was introduced. You do not find that people who are insured against fire are any more careless in throwing lights about than other people. Of course, in some senses, all insurance is open to fraud, and probably always will be. What we do is, as far as possible, to guard against the insurance of Tom, Dick and Harry, and to insure responsible people only. One great protection is that where people claim against us for burglary insurance, they are obliged to make a statutory declaration before a magistrate as to the loss which they have sustained, and persons will think twice before making false declarations, and rendering themselves liable to a prosecution for perjury.

Wood also stressed the advantages to jewellers:

> In the case of a jeweller's shop ... if any light-fingered gentry were to come in and pick up some valuable rings, the loss would be covered. This is a great inducement to jewellers to insure because, as a rule, they are more liable to loss in this way than from burglary, because they usually keep their premises well guarded. Of course the insurance would not include robbery on the part of any person employed by the assured, or loss arising from loot, sack or pillage. It does not cover robbery from the person either, but only from the premises. We might, however, some day try and insure against the former. As showing what is done, we may say we have recently insured a jeweller's shop in Regent Street for over £60,000.

The suggestion that robbery from the person might also be insurable was to prove prophetic. Meanwhile Mr Wood was considerably more specific about the loss at Harringay:

> The lady was out of town, and when the husband got home he found the place had been entered and the jewellery stolen. The claim, however, was only for £22 19s. The policies do not cover any loss which does not amount to £5. Then we also have an average clause in certain policies, to provide that the assured shall only be entitled to recover such proportion of the sum insured as the value of the lost property bears to the total

value covered by insurance. For example, if a man insures at the 2s. 6d. rate for £200, and has goods worth £1,000, he can only recover one-fifth of any loss he may sustain. On the other hand, if a man insures his plate and jewellery only, at 3s. 4d. per cent, and gives a list of the articles insured, with their values, to the underwriter, there is no question about average and the claim will be paid when the loss of the articles is proved.

The *Oracle* reporter's final question to Mr Wood clearly had in mind his women readers. Were there 'a good many lady clients,' he asked, for burglary insurance?

Yes, many ladies nowadays seem to go in fear of burglars, and when they are insured their minds for some reason or other are more at ease. The fear of loss does not frighten them so much as the terror of having burglars in the house; but why the fact of having their property insured should ease their minds it is difficult to say. But it is so, nevertheless. You would be surprised how people are taking the thing up, especially in these autumn days, when the burglary season may be said to have fairly commenced.

One cannot help feeling that the last sentence sent enough shivers down feminine spines in the suburbs to bring a rich harvest of clients to the persuasive Mr Wood. Meanwhile it was becoming a pattern in the market that where Heath led, the companies were quick to follow. In 1889 a Glasgow company, the Mercantile Accident and Guarantee, began covering the risk. Others followed suit, including another Scottish company, the newly-formed General Accident of Perth. By 1903 there were thirty companies involved, producing between them a total premium of over £200,000 for burglary risks. Even so, one major company is said to have so disliked the business that it reinsured its entire burglary account at Lloyd's. The underwriter who wrote it, no doubt with wry amusement, was Cuthbert Heath.

One thing is important to notice about him at this, the height of his almost headlong period of invention. His was the most original talent ever produced by the insurance industry of this or any other country. Yet there was nothing about his urbane temperament that suggested the lonely, pioneering inventor. His true field was the marketplace. Significantly, none of his most truly original ideas were his alone: they almost always stemmed from suggestions made by other people. His flair lay in the fact that he had an unerring way of recognizing a need and was prepared to back his judgement when others were too conformist or too timorous to do so.

A memorable example of this came shortly after his invention of burglary insurance. A woman relative of his lost a piece of jewellery which was covered for burglary under one of his policies. She sent

A fashion plate from *The Queen*, 27 February 1886. It was ladies such as these that Heath's Burglary policy would attract

in a claim, only to be told that accidental loss was not included in the cover. But why, Heath thought, should there not be a policy for loss? The rate would have to be a little higher than that for burglary – say ten shillings per cent. Thus was born the famous 'all risks' policy for jewellery, and it is worth noting that the rate – which Heath conjured out of nothing on the spur of the moment – lasted for half a century.

1890 saw another new policy which had also stemmed from burglary insurance. A book-keeper employed by a Holborn diamond merchant expressed himself concerned about the risk run by his employer while he was carrying his stock round to show his customers. Naturally the diamonds were insured while they were in the merchant's shop – but would it also be possible, the book-keeper wondered, to get some kind of cover on them while the merchant was carrying them, for instance, to his customers in Bond Street? There followed a discussion between the book-keeper and a Lloyd's broker, who put the enquiry, not surprisingly, to Cuthbert Heath's box. The result was another historic policy. Known as the 'jeweller's block' insurance, it has given protection to diamond merchants and jewellers on their travels for nearly a century, and is still underwritten at the Heath box today.

By the time Cuthbert was thirty he had become a man listened to and respected far beyond the market. But if success altered him at all, it did so for the better. 'The Guv'nor' was beginning to be the dominant figure remembered by those who knew him later. 'He was in every way a giant but always a gentle one,' summed up one man who worked closely with him.

The first things most people noticed about him were his height – he was six feet two inches tall – and the black box which contained his deaf-aid. (Later it used to be said at Heath's that any young clerk allowed to carry the famous box was destined for promotion.)

But the impression people carried away was of the rock-like solidity and dominance so powerfully suggested in the Orpen portrait painted in his later years. It was not the only aspect. There is also something about the portrait that suggests a restless drive always seeking a new world to conquer. A slight bulge above his eyebrows suggested intellectual power: it was sufficiently marked to be known in the Heath family as 'the parental bumps'. The eyes themselves – shrewd, penetrating, but always kindly – were deepset in the spare, almost bony features. 'His eyes were very well put in,' recalled one relative, and the phrase sums up the brooding quality about them. He wore a long, slightly drooping but always well-trimmed moustache. In his early days in the Room he would never be seen without a high-wing collar, pearl tiepin and a top hat – except on Fridays, when he wore a bowler. Unlike most underwriters of his time he did not always use a quill: sometimes he used a broad nib.

He was always courteous, notably soft-spoken and immensely kind. Sometimes a young broker who had had a risk turned down would go back to his office, tell his superiors what had happened, and one of the superiors would come back and try to place the risk himself. If at this second attempt Cuthbert was persuaded to write the business, he would never sign the slip for the senior broker. 'Tell your young man to come back and I'll write it,' he would say – the point being that he wanted the young man to have the satisfaction of being the one to get the Heath stamp. There was the same courtesy to younger people on his own box: Bruce Miller, who came to Lloyd's straight from school in 1918, was astounded at being called 'Mr Miller' by Cuthbert.

Fieldsports of all sorts delighted him. But he was never a man of only one dimension. He loved poetry, especially – and perhaps significantly for a deaf man – those most musical of poets, Milton and Swinburne. As to other books, facts intrigued him. He was enthralled by maps, and he would read books on birds, gardens or the history of furniture, but seldom fiction, though he had a taste for Rider Haggard. Birds were a particular enthusiasm, and it seems to have been mutual, for he had a rare gift of attracting them: if a bird was trapped in a room he had only to hold his arm out for it to come and perch there and then let itself be gently carried out.

People who only knew him at his box at Lloyd's would have been amazed to see his water-colours, for which he had far more than a conventional amateur painter's talent. Born in an age when an educated man would take his water-colours on his travels much as a modern traveller takes a camera, he seldom came home from a holiday or a trip abroad without having filled several pages of his sketchbook.

But his paintings of foreign scenes are noticeably less atmospheric than those where he lovingly captures the feeling of the woods and fields round Anstie. One of the best is the picture reproduced on page 140 entitled 'Path to the High Field, Anstie, 1882.' After the title he wrote 'Given to S.G.G.'. The initials were the prelude to an important chapter.

Sarah Caroline Gore Gambier was born in 1859, the daughter of Charles Gore Gambier and his wife Elizabeth. She was a tall, rather commanding-looking girl with dark blue eyes, auburn hair, and a bubbling gaiety and love of parties that was perhaps a reaction to a strict upbringing by her Scottish Lowland mother.

But Sarah was above all a Gambier, and she had inherited the tradition of a family noted for the beauty of its women. Originally springing from Norse seamen who had settled on the Normandy coast, the Gambiers are first recorded as living at Caen in the twelfth century. Prominent Huguenots, they fled to England after the Revocation of the Edict of Nantes in 1685 and proceeded to leave their mark on English history as ambassadors, bankers, judges, but above all as sailors.

Six out of twelve generations of the family produced distinguished naval officers. Two Gambiers are mentioned in the despatch after the Battle of Trafalgar, while an illegitimate son, James Fitzjames, was master of the *Erebus*, the ship which carried Sir John Franklin's

An early marine slip. It bears the names of Cuthbert Heath and the other members of his syndicate. Heath started by writing marine risks but soon moved into the new field of non-marine insurance

Meet of the Surrey Union Foxhounds at Anstie Grange

doomed expedition to the North Pole in 1845. But the most famous of all was Admiral Lord Gambier. Because of his religious fervour he was variously known below decks as Holy Jim or Dismal Jimmy, and was noted for the fact that he forbade alcohol in his flagship, the *Defence*. It did not prevent her being the first ship to break the enemy's line on the Glorious First of June in 1794.

The Heaths and the Gambier families had long been connected by friendship, and also distantly by marriage. Sir William Reid, Sarah's grandfather, had been governor of Malta during the Crimean War, when Lady Heath had lived there in the first year of her marriage. Sir William left a permanent mark of his time in Malta in the form of a fresco, depicting his family, in the Governor's

Sarah Gambier Heath

residence: it replaced another showing 'some lovely but unclad
feminine figures' which had incurred his disapproval.

Thus a web of family connection had drawn Cuthbert and Sarah
together. Later they both recalled how, as children, they used to
play in family cricket matches on the beach at Swanage. Were they
already in love when Cuthbert gave her the water-colour of the Path
to the High Field in 1882? If so, the courtship was a long one, for
they did not become engaged till January 1891 – somewhat un-
seasonably, perhaps, for according to a charming family ritual,
Heath proposals were always made at a particular spot in one of the
rhododendron walks at Anstie. But weddings were in the wind, for
that same month, Cuthbert's brother Herbert was also married.

6 Cadogan Mansions.
Cuthbert Heath's own
water-colour of the
interior of his first
married home

Indeed Cuthbert was the last of Sir Leopold's children to marry. Both his sister Marion and his brother Arthur, now Conservative MP for Louth, had been married in 1881. Frederick, who was in the army, had married his commanding officer's daughter in 1889, while Ada had been married for five years to Harry Broadwood, a partner in the famous firm of piano-makers.

The wedding took place in July, 1891, at Bournemouth. By the following March, Lady Heath noted in her diary, the couple were 'settled in Cadogan Mansions.' Their house was number six: a comfortable, typical house of the period, looking across Sloane Square. Cuthbert used to walk to Lloyd's and back each day from the flat, apparently not so much for the sake of the exercise as because – such were the hierarchic values that persisted in the City – he did not want to meet his clerks on the omnibus. When he did take exercise for pleasure he went riding in the Row. 'Bertie, we heard this morning,' wrote his mother in her diary for 15 July 1895, 'has broken his thigh riding.' It was characteristic that he after-wards became a governor of St George's Hospital where he was taken, and endowed a private room there.

It was at Cadogan Mansions, in 1894, that the Heaths' first child was born and christened Leopold Cuthbert. The flat must have been small for three – especially considering Sarah's zest for giving parties – and in 1897 the Heaths moved to a much larger one on the north side of Portman Square. Over two hundred years old, it had a priest's hole, a chapel, a ghost, and an exceptionally fine Adam ceiling, decorated with what one of the family described as 'mytho-logical ladies joined by loops of flowers.'

Meanwhile the older generation, in the person of Sir Leopold, showed no sign of fading. The Admiral was seventy-one at the time of Cuthbert's marriage. An energetic, spry old man, he still sat on the bench for Dorking district and also seems to have taken his duties seriously at the Hand-in-Hand. These included signing the policies himself, and one of the clerks who used to hold the blotting-paper for Sir Leopold recalled that he used to be treated to a stream of nautical language if he smudged one.

Sir Leopold had also taken to authorship. In 1897, when he was seventy-seven, he published *Letters from the Black Sea*, a vivid record of his Crimean adventures. There was no impairment of his faculties except that – not surprisingly after all his campaigns – he was a little gun-deaf. One of his relations recalls that it used to be said in the family that Sir Leopold and Cuthbert would be seen cheerfully chatting together in the Dorking-London train when other people's conversation was silenced by noisy tunnels. The suggestion that Cuthbert had some ability to lip-read is supported by a recollection of Mr Bruce Miller, who worked closely with him at the box, that 'strangely enough I could always make him hear if I turned round to face him.' The ability seems to have been uncon-scious, for his daughter Genesta recalls her mother becoming 'mildly irritated' at his persistent refusal to learn to lip-read.

Meanwhile Douglas Denon Heath had died in 1897 at Kitlands. During his later years – he lived to be eighty-six – he had occupied himself with the welfare of the people of Coldharbour, and with contributing occasional articles to learned publications. Earlier, speaking of his editing of Lord Bacon's legal remains, he had said, 'I dare not expect a single soul will read my work, but I thought it rather well done.' It is a sad but not unworthy epitaph for this gentle, solitary and dedicated man. He was buried at Coldharbour with, as he had characteristically wished, 'a simple funeral, no trumpery.' His uncle's death had one notable consequence for Cuthbert. In 1893 his mother's diary mentions that he and Sarah had 'a little hunting-box at Horsham'. Country life was always a necessity for Cuthbert: later in his life there were times when almost every letter he wrote from Anstie would speak of his joy of being out of London.

But Horsham is some little way from Dorking, and for Cuthbert the country meant, and only meant, the beloved Leith Hill acres. Now, with Douglas Heath's death, Kitlands had passed to Sir Leopold. Cuthbert made an arrangement to rent the house from his father, and he and Sarah moved there in 1897. Two years later came another important event: the birth of his daughter Genesta. The name, unusual and graceful as it is, was actually a mistake. *Genista* is the name of a variety of broom which flourishes on Mont St Michel where Sarah Heath grew up – but spelling, according to her daughter, was not Sarah's strong point.

Thus by the turn of the century Cuthbert's home life was complete, with his wife, his son and daughter, his homes at Portman Square and Kitlands. As to his business, the new century was to ring in a new age of underwriting.

Throughout his life Cuthbert Heath remained faithful to certain basic principles of underwriting. On the one hand he was always positive in his approach to a risk, and as to the rates, he knew his intuition would seldom fail him. It was, recalls one former Heaths' underwriter, Eric Squire,

> the *basis* of an insurance contract that he was adamant about. That is to say he required his premium to be calculated on a rate which was related directly to the risk exposure. For material damage such as fire and burglary, he required the amount insured to be subject to the average clause, so that the policy would pay the same proportion of the loss as the policy amount bore to the value of the insured property at the time of the loss. Similarly when he insured an intangible risk such as Third Party or Fidelity, he would relate his rate to the payroll or the turnover, or some such criterion whereby the greater the exposure, the greater the premium would automatically be.

Meanwhile the new and uncharted world of non-marine insurance presented new problems. Suppose an underwriter had insured fifty buildings in a city in South America – if that city was hit by a hurricane, an earthquake, or ravaged by a major fire such as that which destroyed 12,000 buildings in Chicago in 1871, he would face a massive list of claims all arising from the one disaster. In such cases a factual method of assessing rates was needed, and Cuthbert's first essay in doing so was based on hurricane statistics. He and his friend Christopher Head set methodically to work,

Cuthbert and Sarah
Heath

St. Kitts (N. Indies) Equake 5/
                         T.W   2/6

Gales + Hurricanes
   Bldgs of £500 or over in value   12/6
      "   " £200   "   "   "   17/6
      "   under £200 "   "   "   30/
   ex of 5% or £25

St. Lucia (N. Indies)   Equake 10/
                          T.W   2/6
Gales + Hurricanes same as St Kitts.

St. Vincent (N. Indies)   Equake 10/
                            T.W   2/6
                   Equake + T.W. 20/
Gales + Hurricanes same as St Kitts.

St. Thomas (N. Indies)   Equake 10/
                           T.W   2/6
Gales + Hurricanes same as St Kitts.

Surinan (Dutch Guiana)   Equake 2/6
                         T.W   2/6

Seattle (U.S.A)   Equake 10/-

Salina Cruz (Mexico)   Equake 1?

San Blas. (Mexico)   Equake 5

Santiago (Chile)   Equake 2

San Salvador (Salvador)   Equake ?

San Francisco (U.S.A)
        Equake
           (a) Concrete-Steel Bldg   1
           (b) others   2

San Remo (Riviera)
        Equake
           (a) Villas on Rock   5
           (b) Hotels

Smyrna   Equake (brick + stone) ?
         Same as Constantinople

The Earthquake Book. Cuthbert Heath was the first underwriter to compile detailed statistics relating to the risks he wrote

beginning with a collection of maps which showed the course of every West Indies hurricane over the last hundred years. It was comparatively easy, Cuthbert noted, to fix the amount of damage which might be expected to arise from one hurricane. But it was also important to discover to what extent particular trees or crops would be affected by it. This varied because of the different seasons when the crops became mature. 'But in the end,' he wrote, 'we were able to obtain a good grasp of the subject and to fix rates which one way in with the other have proved profitable.'

The next step was to do the same for earthquakes. Cuthbert and Christopher Head made an intensive study of what they found was 'the considerable literature' connected with the subject. Soon they were buying up maps which marked all recorded catastrophes in specific countries: the maps were evidently rare, for Cuthbert paid a hundred guineas for one which showed Indian earthquakes. Another source was the record kept by the Jesuit fathers on the west coast of America in the fifteenth century, while for China there were records going back two thousand years. 'The curious thing about earthquake hazards is that the inhabitants of the areas affected by them live in a state of optimism,' Cuthbert concluded, and went on to describe his own experience relating to the Jamaican earthquake of 1907:

> Our rate for Kingston, Jamaica, founded on the previous history of the island and of certain parts of it in particular, was fixed at 10s.%. Scarcely anybody would pay it, and when the Earthquake did occur I do not think we had an insurance on our books. Naturally after the Earthquake there was no absence of business, and people were content to pay double what we had previously suggested.

The earthquake book, not quite in its original form, is still kept at one of the Heath boxes at Lloyd's. The task of copying Christopher Head's original version was one of the first tasks given to George Thomson – later to be chairman of Lloyd's – when he started work at Heath's in 1914. The copy, Mr Thomson recalls, was given by Cuthbert Heath to a friend in one of the companies – not because he wanted his rivals to benefit from his expertise, but, characteristically, because he did not want them to undercut his rates.

But perhaps the most significant point about the earthquake book is that it demonstrates yet another way in which Cuthbert Heath was shaping the path of modern underwriting. Before his time, insurance men had been simple men of business. Since his time they have become experts in whatever field of technology they cover: it is part of the legacy of Cuthbert Heath that a modern contemporary underwriter of, say, nuclear power stations is able to talk on more or less equal terms with a nuclear scientist.

Meanwhile there were other important foundations to be built on. From his earliest days at Lloyd's his mother had spoken of Cuthbert 'getting rich with brokerage'. Probably these early broking activities were of an informal kind, but in 1890 he seems to have formed a broking partnership designed to feed his syndicate with business. Though the conception was very different from that of a modern broking house which places business throughout the market, it was another landmark, for it was the beginning of C. E. Heath and Co., Insurance Brokers.

In 1894 there came a more startling departure. In that year the premium income of the Heath syndicate was rather less than £100,000 – a formidable sum in terms of the growing strength of the non-marine market, but small in terms of the risks he was now being asked to cover. Even though he was writing for other syndicates besides his own, Heath needed more capacity. And in 1894 he had taken the step – unheard of among Lloyd's underwriters – of forming his own insurance company. This is Cuthbert's own account of how it came into being:

> Feeling that non-marine business was growing and would grow at Lloyd's, I went to the Committee of the day, or its Chairman, I forget which, and proposed that the Committee should accept a deposit from me to cover my non-marine business. The Committee declined, saying they were only concerned with marine business. I therefore formed the Excess Insurance Company which with a capital of £5,000 fully paid up was used as a backing for two of my names, every risk being reinsured with it. Inasmuch as the Capital was practically held by these two names it was taking the place of a deposit.

The Excess Company's stated objects were to write marine, fire and accident business and reinsurance. It was also to specialize in Fidelity – the branch of insurance which indemnifies an employer against fraud by his employees. Another important area was Workmen's Compensation. Since the Employers' Liability Act of 1880, there had sprung up a huge new market in insuring employers who now found themselves for the first time legally liable for accidents to their workpeople.

Strictly speaking, it was against the rules of the committee of Lloyd's for company business to be written in the Room. Later Cuthbert was to deny all knowledge of this rule, but the insurance correspondent of the *Journal of Commerce* may have been nearer the facts when he described how Cuthbert had found an ingenious means by which the rules could be complied with:

> At first Mr Heath wrote a line for a syndicate of two names, his own and that of his cousin, Mr George Heath. On the back of the Lloyd's policy, signed by these two names, was printed a policy of the Excess, reinsuring the whole of the risk, and in this manner the disability of the prohibition of a company transacting business in the Room was overcome.

Later, as we shall see, this was to bring rumblings from the committee of Lloyd's. Meanwhile his next move was to bring insurance in a new and dramatic way before the public.

Every generation has its special hazards and anxieties, and in the late August days of 1901 *The Times* reported 'a sudden increase' in the number of smallpox cases in the London area. The increase continued ominously through the first week of September, and as it went on, the more far-seeing tried to encourage vaccination. On 12 September a case was reported from a place called Five Oak Green, near Tonbridge: it was a hamlet famous for its hopfields, and the victim was one of the huge bands of East Enders who every

Hospital steam ships *Albert Victor, Geneva Cross,* and *Maltese Cross* which were set up as inoculation centres on the Thames during the 1901 smallpox epidemic

autumn made the Kentish countryside the scene of a riproaring fiesta. In order to encourage vaccination, the resourceful curate of St Augustine's Church, Stepney, who was accompanying a party from his parish, organized what were called 'vaccination concerts' in a marquee on the village green, the idea being that people could be persuaded to get themselves vaccinated in special tents during the intervals. Probably such ideas did something to reduce the spread of infection, but it was not enough. By 17 September, 132 cases of smallpox were reported in the London area. By the end of October the total had steadied at around 200, but new cases were still being reported daily.

As usual, and especially because the outbreak had begun among East Enders, it was the poor who bore the brunt. For one case a day reported from Kensington, there were eight from Stepney. Soon special isolation hospitals had been set up at South Wharf, Rotherhithe, and in the grim setting of two isolation ships, the *Atlas* and *Endymion*, moored off Long Reach in the river.

Even so nobody could feel safe. The only way of preventing epidemics, proclaimed one advertisement for a firm in Long Acre, was to use 'Merryweather's Chlorus Distributor for disinfecting courts and alleys'. Another product, Merryweather's Hydraulic

Sewer Flusher, would, it was claimed, clean drains with one-tenth of the water normally used for the purpose.

Such devices were candles in the wind. The grim roll-call climbed steadily through November and December, reaching 800 by early January. The thousand mark was reached before the end of the month. By March the total was 1,500, with upwards of forty new cases being reported daily.

Possibly Cuthbert recalled the cholera outbreak when he was seven, and how, even in such a safe zone as Leith Hill, the Heath children had been forbidden water and put on a gooseberry ration. Certainly he was quick to realize that at a time of anxiety, people needed some kind of talisman, and the talisman could be insurance. Like the curate of St Augustine's, he was a firm believer in vaccination, and before long he was insuring individuals against getting the disease at a rate of 2s. 6d. per cent, with the proviso that the assured must have been vaccinated. Thus anyone who paid £1 in premium would, if he got the disease, receive £800. 'News of this novel form of insurance,' said one observer,

> reached the daily papers and immediately Lloyd's brokers were inundated with orders varying from amounts running into thousands of pounds to the humble £100 of the city clerk. So great was the rush that brokers sent juniors to keep a place in the queue at Mr Heath's box immediately Lloyd's opened, arriving later in the day with piles of 'slips' hastily prepared for the morning's orders. Mr Heath drafted every available clerk from his office into his box, with power to write without limit. If, however, the residence of the assured was in a locality from which a case of smallpox had been reported, the rate was increased to 3s. 9d. per cent, and if further cases were reported from that locality the rate rose to 5s. per cent.

Cuthbert made a small fortune from his smallpox underwriting. But there was a more important aspect. His insistence on vaccination sounded the first note of a new theme in insurance – the concept that what is good for the insurer is also good for the community in general. Years ahead of his time as usual, he was guiding the market towards the modern science of risk prevention.

It was one of the consequences of Cuthbert's good nature that in the course of his life he spent a great deal of time and trouble in helping those less talented in the handling of business affairs than he was. This was never so fully demonstrated as in the case of John Broadwoods, the piano-makers.

His interest in this historic firm arose through his sister Ada, who had now been married for fourteen years to one of the partners

in the firm, Harry Broadwood, whose father, Henry Fowler Broadwood, owned extensive estates a few miles from Anstie on the
Surrey-Sussex border.

Broadwoods' history went back to 1728, when a young Swiss
named Burkat Shudi had started making harpsichords in London.
In 1761 he had been joined by John Broadwood, a young Scots
cabinet-maker who had walked to London from the Borders to
seek his fortune. Broadwood became not only Shudi's assistant
but his son-in-law: as a result of marrying Shudi's daughter
Barbara, he came eventually to inherit the business.

For its first 150 years Broadwoods was as commercially successful as its tradition was romantic. Its name was synonymous with
piano-making of the highest quality. Not only could it claim to
have supplied harpsichords to Handel, Mozart and Haydn and to
have given a piano to Beethoven, but in 1840 it employed 400
workmen and was listed as being among the twelve top firms in
London. Nelson and Wellington had been customers and so were
the royal family. To this day the firm lists on its notepaper every
monarch from George II to the present Queen, whom it still supplies
under Royal Warrant.

Such was the firm in which Harry Broadwood had become a
partner in 1879, after coming down from Cambridge. Unhappily
for him, its future prospects were then begining to appear a good

The Shudi family of
harpsichord makers
into which John
Broadwood married

deal less rosy than its splendid history. The next twenty years, writes Mr David Wainwright, the historian of Broadwoods,

> were to see the erosion of the British pianoforte market, from two main causes – the introduction of new technology, and the development of American and German pianos. The new technology involved overstringing, a system of carrying the longer strings across the shorter instead of keeping the strings in parallel; and the full cast iron frame (an innovation that took the American piano makers, particularly Steinway, into world leadership on the concert platforms.) Harry's father, Henry Fowler Broadwood, set his face against both innovations.

Over the next twenty years Broadwoods faced competition not only from Steinways but from Continental firms such as Bluthner and Bechstein which began to capture even the traditional English markets, while new British firms making cheaper pianos helped to challenge Broadwoods' long-established dominance. In the later 1890s there were problems over renewing the lease of their factory in Westminster. The firm's profits began to drop in the face of ever-fiercer competition, and though Broadwoods made 1500 pianos in 1900, the result of their trading was a loss. Matters seem not to have been helped by family friction among the Broadwoods: Harry Broadwood, according to his daughter Mrs Edwin Wood, 'quarrelled with one of his uncles, who wanted his money out of the firm when things were going badly.'

Cuthbert with his daughter Genesta in France about 1903

It was at this point that Cuthbert Heath stepped in. His motive, says Mr Wainwright, 'was obviously his affection for his sister Ada.' In October 1901 the former partnership was dissolved. John Broadwood and Sons was formed as a new company and, with Cuthbert's help, capital was supplied to build a new factory at Hackney. The new board members he introduced were men who brought civilized tastes to the firm as well as money. Cuthbert's nominee as chairman was another Lloyd's underwriter, William Leslie, the son of a well-known conductor of Victorian times: an enthusiastic amateur musician himself, Leslie's name still survives in the Lloyd's broking house of Leslie and Godwin. Another director was William Spottiswoode, the publisher and another keen amateur musician.

Though Broadwoods were thus set on their feet by Cuthbert, it was not the end of the story of the help he gave them; as late as 1923 we find the Excess Company making a loan of £9,000 to Broadwoods. (The auditors, questioning the value of the investment, noted that it made a total over the years of £40,000.) What mattered more to Cuthbert than the £40,000 was that Broadwoods always stood high in his affections. No one would have rejoiced more that the firm is still a client of Heaths, or at the fact that several members of the present-day company were present at a dinner at the Savoy in 1978, held to celebrate Broadwoods' 250 years of history.

It may be reassuring for the modern underwriter to know that not everything turned to gold at Cuthbert's touch. One of his contemporaries, Arthur Rose, recalled seeing 'a quantity of policy forms to cover risk of burst pipes from frost. The idea was from Germany where cold is intense.' Rose found that the policy had been drawn up by a broking firm named Waltons, 'chiefly in conjunction with C. E. H., who was prepared to take the risk. But the scheme came to nothing in our milder winters.'

One supposed lapse of judgment which has often been remarked on is that Cuthbert did not see the possibilities of – or at least did not persist with – Pluvius insurance, which is today used to cover everything from garden fêtes to Grands Prix against cancellation because of bad weather. The scheme is said to have been devised by a Heath underwriter named Robert Gambles, and certainly it was written at the Heath box early in the century. Later Heath turned the business over to the Eagle Star, together with Gambles who joined the company to run it. The episode was mentioned in one of Cuthbert's obituaries as his most striking failure, but Mr Eric Squire has pointed out that the true explanation is that he simply found the business unworkable in a Lloyd's syndicate. 'Mr Heath handed the business over to the Eagle Star,' says Mr Squire, 'because as a company they had a network of local agents who could carry out the vitally necessary exercise of reading the rain-gauges which showed whether claims were justified. He could rely on no such network.'

Meanwhile the fledgling non-marine market inevitably had other problems, among them an unprofitable attempt to cover Southern European farmers against hail damage, and a South African property insurance which made substantial losses in the Boer War. Probably both contributed to some lean underwriting results for the Heath syndicate from 1897 to 1900: the average profits paid to each name had been £702 in 1896, but in 1897 the syndicate had made a loss, with only marginal profits for the next three years. By 1901 they were back to a respectable £645. In 1902 – presumably helped by the smallpox profits – they reached £857.

Three years later he had evidently returned £2,000 of the original £7,000 his father had given him when he first started underwriting, for under an agreement drawn up by Sir Leopold in November 1905, Cuthbert promised to give his father the interest from the invest-

The San Francisco earthquake. The magnanimous attitude of Lloyd's underwriters to the disaster was a cornerstone of their American reputation

ment of the remaining £5,000, 'and to give me [Sir Leopold] also after taking to yourself £150, each year four-fifths of the net profit of the underwriting. You also agree to give to me during my life time all those profits arising from the share standing in your name in Head's syndicate.' Cuthbert's immediate affairs were clearly prospering – but the real achievement he could now look to was that he had, with almost nonchalant ease, woken Lloyd's from its long sleep and begun to build the modern market.

Meanwhile there was another point. The early days of the non-marine market – 'the Elizabethan age of Lloyd's underwriting' as Gibb, the Lloyd's historian, has called them – had coincided with the first stirrings of a new giant buyer of insurance. In the first decade of the century America was reaching a new peak of prosperity, and its insurance needs did not begin to be met by the domestic markets. In 1899 a Lloyd's broker touring the United States had found enough business in a few months to bring him £1,000 a year commission, and by now the demand was many times greater. From Cape Cod to California a vast new market was opening up. New York jewellers needed insurance, so did the banks, and so did the rugged bosses of the Chicago stockyards. It was in the new Lloyd's market that they, and the rest of booming America, began to seek it.

Moreover the reputation of British insurers stood extremely high. The Chicago fire of 1871 had been followed by another at Boston a year later. This time the damage was £15 million, of which the British market paid out £1 million, 'honouring its debts', notes George Clayton, 'with a promptness which drew nothing but admiration from the American public.'

But the Chicago and Boston fires were only the prelude to an event which still ranks among the greatest catastrophes of insurance history. On 18 April 1906, at twelve minutes past five in the morning, a geological fissure on the west coast of America known as the San Andreas fault slipped over a segment of 270 miles. The resulting shock was felt from Los Angeles to Oregon, but the main damage was to the city of San Francisco, where 30,000 houses were demolished. Seven hundred people were killed by the earthquake and by the fire which almost immediately followed. The total underwriting loss was £45 million, of which the British share was nearly a quarter. The Heath syndicate, as leaders on Lloyd's earthquake policies, faced enormous losses.

It was many months before all the claims could be unravelled. Some policies covered fire only, others earthquake only, and others fire if caused by earthquake. Several continental insurers made the point that fire insurance policies could not be held to cover fires caused by an earthquake, and many in fact repudiated claims on this ground. American domestic companies were among the worst hit. Philip Heath has recalled being told by Cuthbert how 'lawyers employed by American companies descended on the City with the express purpose of avoiding payment of as many claims as possible.' Such methods were not for him. He simply sent a cable to his San Francisco agent: 'Pay all our policy-holders in full irrespective of the terms of their policies.'

Even today American insurance men will tell you that Lloyd's owes its reputation in the United States to that historic gesture.

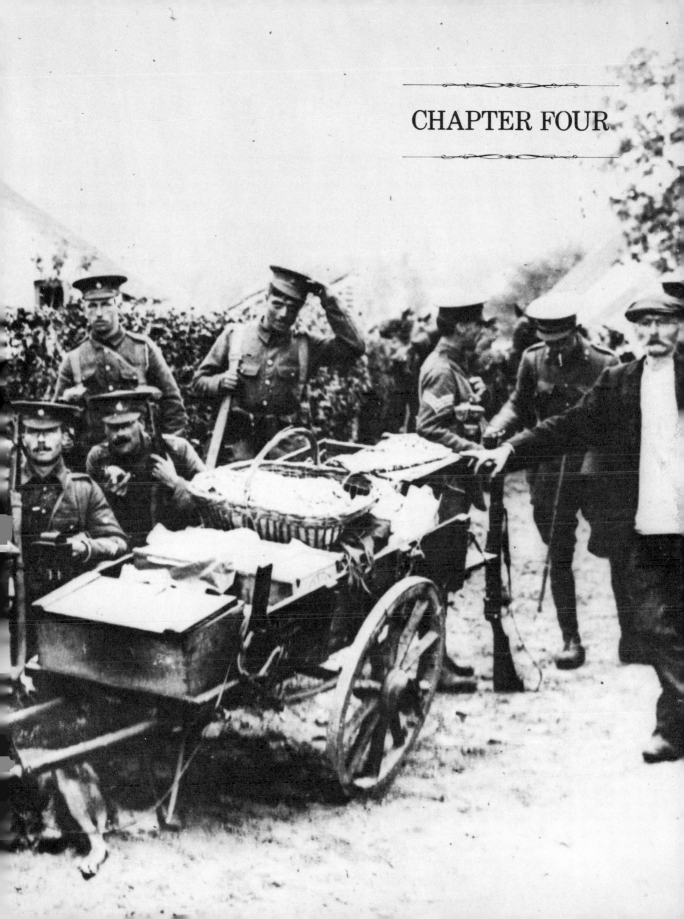

CHAPTER FOUR

The Years of Influence

From the public's point of view the test of any insurer is whether he is able to pay legitimate claims. His solvency is the touchstone of his professional existence.

Cuthbert Heath's creation of non-marine insurance at Lloyd's had probably saved the market from extinction. But in other ways it had helped to highlight the problem of the solvency of Lloyd's insurers. Before 1908 there was no requirement on an underwriter, apart from a deposit of £5,000, which made it certain he could pay his claims. And as syndicates grew larger, the greater was the cash-flow to them. This in turn tempted some of the more optimistic – or less scrupulous – underwriters to invest premium which properly belonged to their names in some none too certain projects.

Another factor was that the growth of non-marine business had led to the writing of all kinds of risks by people who were, as Gibb put it, 'trying to emulate Heath but deficient in his underwriting genius'. Under the Lloyd's Act of 1871 there was no provision for a member's deposits to be used to cover anything except marine risks: according to the letter of the law, the writing of non-marine risks was entirely unofficial. Heath himself had persistently tried to persuade the committee of Lloyd's to accept a non-marine deposit from him, but their answer had always been that the marine-orientated terms of the Lloyd's Act made it impossible for them to do so. However in 1902 they had reluctantly allowed him to put up a deposit of £2,000.

As far as the market as a whole was concerned, the decision seems to have been a case of too little and too late. For that same year saw one of Lloyd's more resounding failures. This involved an underwriter named Burnand, who had speculated freely with his names' money in a travel agency of which he was a director. One of the travel agency's problems was that it had bought a large number of seats for King Edward's Coronation. When this was postponed because of the King's ill-health, the agency lost the money it had invested. Burnand then borrowed money from the banks, pledging the resources of his underwriting agency. Things went steadily downhill for him, and eventually it was found that he had made his unfortunate names responsible for debts which amounted to £100,000.

PREVIOUS PAGE British troops in Belgium at the beginning of the First World War

The good name of Lloyd's duly suffered – but how was it possible for so individualistic an organization to prevent similar happenings in the future? For several years it had been suggested that the committee of Lloyd's should find a way of stopping premiums being misused. The most effective of the suggested ways, it seemed, was some kind of audit or annual review which would guarantee that an underwriter was always in a position to meet his liabilities.

Cuthbert Heath himself was to take a revolutionary step in this direction. In those days it was the practice for one underwriter to issue a policy to another which promised to bail him out in time of trouble. In 1906 Heath added a proviso. He refused to sign a guarantee policy for a fellow-member unless the member had first submitted his accounts to a rigorous audit of Cuthbert's own devising. At the time the step seems to have gone largely unnoticed – except perhaps for a few grumbles from those whose accounts would not have stood examination. For most people in the market, any idea of a general audit smacked of an unwarrantable intrusion.

Meanwhile the effects of the Burnand troubles smouldered on Over the next few years there were several more failures of underwriters nonc sensational enough to create a scandal on the Burnand scale, but the general feeling of unease was spreading. The motoring press warned its readers not to insure at Lloyd's, and the market's reputation in America was so badly dented that Lloyd's began taking advertisement space in US papers to remind people how it had paid up on San Francisco.

Possibly Lloyd's might have ridden out this period of rough weather as it had done before and has done since. But in July 1908, following more whispers of insolvencies, a reproach came from a more authoritative quarter. For several years now *The Times* had run a regular series of reports from Lloyd's, which were written by an extremely competent financial journalist named Harcourt Kitchin.

Kitchin was well known in the market, where he had made a point of cultivating underwriters likely to produce a story. It was also a two-way traffic: if an underwriter wanted his views publicly aired, Kitchin was a willing and useful mouthpiece. One of his close acquaintances was Sidney Boulton, a member of the committee and a leader, with Heath, of what may be called the reform group. And what now was to put a match to the slow burning fuse of unrest was an article by Kitchin, which was almost certainly inspired by Boulton.

It appeared on 17 July, at the head of the leader column of the special business supplement which the paper in those days published weekly. Beginning with a handsome tribute to Lloyd's – its

service to the public, the leader said, could 'hardly be over-rated' –
it moved on to the essence of the problem:

> Nobody knows, except the members of a syndicate, how its funds are
> invested. They may be used for speculative purposes on the Stock Ex-
> change or in the produce markets. Cases, in fact, have been known
> where funds have been used in this way, and money has been lost. As
> compared with the large sums which should be readily available to meet
> liabilities of large syndicates for unexpired risks, it must be owned that
> the amount of the official deposits is insignificant.

The attack, underwriters must have felt as they read the leader,
was the stronger for its moderate, temperate expression. It was
also, they found as they read on, constructive:

> We believe that the public would be satisfied if the underwriting syndi-
> cates had properly audited balance sheets prepared every year, and sub-
> mitted them privately to the committee of Lloyd's.
> The mere fact that such a balance sheet had to be submitted would
> automatically compel underwriters to make sure that all their liabili-
> ties for unexpired risks were provided for and their funds properly
> invested ... We believe that the credit of underwriting members would
> again become practically invulnerable if they took the necessary step
> to secure a semi-private audit.

Evidently the committee had had advance warning of the contents of the leader – probably from Boulton who, being on the
committee himself, would have felt it proper to tell his fellow-
members. At least a fortnight previously, they must have taken
steps to consider the possibility of setting up an audit, for on 12
July they received a legal opinion that was sweepingly against the
concept. The opinion was that it was 'not within the powers of the
Corporation of Lloyd's to guarantee its members as proposed. To
act as a Guarantee Society . . . is quite foreign to the scope of the
Act which incorporates the Society.' To put such a proposal into
effect, the lawyer's letter added, would need an Act of Parliament.
This forthright legal salvo cannot have made things easier for the
Chairman of Lloyd's, Sir John Luscombe, beset as he was on the
one hand by the growing number of reformers, and on the other by
the stalwarts of the old guard who regarded all talk of an audit as
intolerable interference.

Clearly Luscombe and the committee had to act. A reproach from
The Times could hardly be ignored, and a meeting of underwriters
was called for 24 July. Luscombe's own feelings seem to have
been ambiguous, but all the same he contrived to inject a note of
urgency into the proceedings: for on that very day, he told the

assembled underwriters, perhaps at that very moment, a large railway company which had always placed its insurances at Lloyd's was meeting to consider whether to instruct its brokers to place the business elsewhere. What was now proposed, he said, was the forming of a special committee to look into the possibility of what would be, in effect, an audit. The meeting seems to have been relieved at the thought that the matter might thus be, as one underwriter put it in relaxed schoolboy style, 'thrashed out over the holidays' and the proposal, which committed no one, was agreed to. Cuthbert Heath was to be on the special committee.

Till now the running on the pro-audit side had mostly come from Boulton. But now, as the special committee addressed itself to the technical problems of the audit, it was Heath's advice it wanted: he, after all, had introduced a pilot scheme of his own and made it work. The rest of the committee were like men planning an expedition to an undiscovered land – while he had actually been there.

Fundamentally the solvency test which Heath had applied over

Cuthbert Heath's Audit 'manifesto' which he drew up in 1908 to persuade the Committee of Lloyd's to set up a means of control of individual syndicates whereby they could protect the public and Lloyd's reputation his guarantee was rigorous but simple. It was based on an under-writer's previous years. Lloyd's results, then as now, were calculated three years in arrears – the point being that this gave an extra margin of safety by allowing for losses not reported or claimed on till the third year. Heath's system, explains Gibb,

> had solved the difficulty by making an underwriter's past years the yard-stick for his present underwriting. The auditor was told to look back at a man's figures for the last three 'closed' years and find out from them what percentage of the year's premium income had been settled at the end of the first year of an account; what percentage at the end of the second; and what percentage at the end of the third. The percentages of these closed years must then be applied to the open years as they came under the audit.

By the end of October the special committee had virtually adopted the Heath scheme for the market as a whole. Now, at another meeting called for 3 November, they faced the reaction of the market. Since July there had been a slight swing towards reform but the result was by no means certain: even a close associate of Boulton himself still described the idea of the audit as 'inquisitorial, oppressive, offensive, and disgustingly insulting'.

Thanks to Heath, the special committee had got the expertise they needed – they knew, and could prove to others, that the audit system worked. Heath's expertise had made a major contribution but now, a day or so before the crucial meeting, he showed a different kind of authority – no longer merely technical but moral. He knew that Lloyd's future probably depended on the decision of the meeting on 3 November. Somehow the wind must be taken from the opposition's sails. Perhaps the nautical metaphor is not out of place: his actions now showed the attacking skill he would have brought to bear on his opponents had he become, as he had once dreamed, an admiral like his father.

What Heath did has become memorable in the annals of Lloyd's. He wrote, in his own hand on a piece of foolscap, two sentences. They read as follows:

> We, the undersigned underwriting members would agree to hand in to the Committee of Lloyd's annually a statement, signed by an approved accountant, that we were in possession of assets reasonably sufficient to wind up our underwriting accounts.
>
> We suggest that a Committee should be appointed to consider the best method of carrying out the above proposal.

To this he obtained the signatures of forty-two leading under-writers. Characteristically, he did not put his own name at the top:

the original, preserved among Lloyd's most historic documents, shows that he did not sign till half a dozen others had done so first.

Gibb, who was fond of Biblical metaphors, saw the brilliance of Heath's move as making a division of the sheep and goats among the underwriters:

> The list was there for anybody to sign ... Anyone who liked could add his name to it and by doing so secure himself a place in the fold. But if he refused to sign, if he declared openly that he would not undergo an audit or provide a certificate, if in a word he took his place among the goats, what would be thought of him? His obstinacy would be taken for nervousness about his own solvency. Cautious brokers with good risks to place would fight shy of him. Prudent merchants and shipowners would tell their brokers to do business only with audited names.

Despite Heath's pre-emptive strike a few doubts remained among the diehards. They were finally scattered after an effective speech at the meeting by one member, F. A. White, who told the meeting that *The Times* leader had now been reprinted in the world's press from Canada to China. He reminded the members how Burnand had 'squandered' his premiums and then proposed an amendment that, as well as the audit, a trust fund should be established. The audit proposal and the amendment were put to the meeting and both were unanimously carried.

Three days later *The Times*, magnanimously underplaying its own part in the affair, congratulated Lloyd's on having set its house in order. In a leader called 'The Strengthening of Lloyd's' it declared that:

> The new arrangements are strict, and it is even possible that before they come into effect they may be made severer: one thing is certain, namely, that Lloyd's underwriters are determined that isolated cases of weakness shall not again bring into question the fair name of the 'Room'.

After the critical events of the autumn, things proceeded smoothly and also swiftly. On 23 December, all syndicates were told that they must return their audit certificates within three months.

In the end, even those who had opposed the audit found some consolation. Under the new Insurance Act of 1911 the government had planned to demand a deposit of £2,000 from all Lloyd's non-marine underwriters, but because of the existence of the audit this was eventually waived. Two years later a second Lloyd's Act was passed. Under it, the protection of the 1871 Act – which had been for marine policies only – now included non-marine as well.

Thus the market which Cuthbert Heath had invented now reached

full stature. But the truly momentous crisis had been the battle of
the audit. Even if he had never done anything else for Lloyd's, his
pre-eminence in its history would be secure – on the strength of two
sentences written on a single sheet of foolscap paper.

By 1907 Heath was writing for twenty names, and business on his
syndicate was booming. One reason for this was that his attitude
over the San Francisco earthquake had redounded to the credit of
the London market, and helped Cuthbert himself to show a dramatic
rise in profits. The syndicate's average profits per name in 1906
had been £431. Now, largely as a result of the improved rates on
earthquake business, they had risen to £1,435.

It was a remarkable result when one considers the small scale of
the enterprise in those days. In 1906 the Heath office in Winchester
House, on the corner of Old Broad Street and London Wall, consisted of only fifteen people, of whom two were brokers: another
two were members of the Excess staff. Robert North, later the
company secretary, has described the hazards of telephone com-
munication in the office:

> We had one candlestick telephone in the office – in the passage – and,
> when the bell rang, Mr Heath used to shout out 'Boy' which was usually
> me. In fear and trembling I had to listen to all kinds of abstruse insur-
> ance talk which was Greek to me, and relay it to Mr Heath who stood
> behind me and growled out the answers which I had to transmit to the
> caller. What with Mr Heath's rather indistinct pronunciation, the tech-
> nical terms used in the conversation at both ends, my natural nervous-
> ness, and the poor transmission in those early telephone days, I some-
> times wonder what kind of misunderstandings arose as a result of these
> calls.

Shortly after 1906, North recalled, the staff increased 'fairly
rapidly' after the San Francisco earthquake. But another consequence of the disaster was also to affect the wider market. Some
of the great American companies had been alarmed by the failure
of other insurers to pay their losses. With a view to finding means
to cover such catastrophes in future, the Hartford Fire Insurance
Company sent representatives to London, seeking a means to
protect themselves from the results of a single San Francisco-type
disaster.

The great insurance companies like the Hartford were not
troubled with the run-of-the-mill fires which every insurance
company must expect. They wanted protection against an event
which might destroy half a city where large numbers of householders and business men would be their clients. So Heath devised
what he called excess of loss cover. Under it the direct insurer

would retain the responsibility for all the smaller losses himself. Larger losses above an agreed maximum figure would be paid by the reinsurer up to a second agreed limit, after which the liability reverted to the original insurer, who could then buy further re-insurances for the upper limits. As a further sophistication of the system, the reinsurer could himself buy reinsurance – known as a retrocession – in respect of the responsibilities he now assumed.

Meanwhile the range of non-marine insurance as a whole was growing. An important new area was Workmen's Compensation: following the original Employers' Liability Act of 1880, the first Workmen's Compensation Act of 1897 had laid down that an employer was responsible for accidents at work even if these were not caused by his negligence. Only the more dangerous occupations were covered at first, but by 1906 the Act was made applicable to every sort of workman. Lloyd George was President of the Board of Trade at the time, and Cuthbert was called in for consultations about clauses embodied in the Bill in the interests of insurers. When the Act came into force there was a rush of employers to take out the liability cover which, in the earliest days, was only available from the Heath syndicate. Cuthbert was 'remonstrated with' by the chairman of Lloyd's, he later recalled, because the queue of brokers wanting to place the business stretched from his box right into the Reading Room.

One of the most historic documents in the Heath archives is Lloyd's first American motor policy. It is dated 1907, and it covered a steam car built by the White Sewing Machine Company of Chicago. But still more important to the story of Heaths is that the policy came to Lloyd's through the firm of Rollins Burdick Hunter.

This famous Chicago broking house had been founded in 1897 in the great expanding age of American insurance. Its first significant link with Heaths came in 1908 when Charles Rollins, its founder, visited London with a view to placing some high-risk insurances for the big Chicago meatyards. Chicago was then the world's meat-packing centre, and the factories and yards owned by Rollins' clients often extended over many acres. One incidental aspect of their business was that boxes were needed for packing the meat, and in order to make the boxes, some leading firms had set up their own sawmills. The fire risks on such properties were high, and premium rates were often as much as twelve per cent.

Soon Cuthbert Heath was writing not only this high-risk business for the meatyards, but a host of other policies that Rollins brought him. In 1912 he wrote one of the first fleets of American trucks, and the first auto fleet for a meat-packing company came around the same time. Another policy that broke fresh ground

LLOYD'S MOTOR CAR INSURANCE POLICY.

Whereas   E.J. Gutmann

of   Chicago, Illinois

No. 0001

hereinafter called the Assured, ~~has~~ have paid { 50.00   Premium   difference in exchange }

Premium or Consideration to Us, who have hereunto subscribed our Names to insure against loss as follows, viz.:—

£ 500

Upon GASOLINE ELECTRIC STEAM Automobile No. 3556

$2500

Make   White Sewing Machine Co.   while in the United States, Canada, and Western Europe, also other places when agreed to by endorsement hereon

Only against the Risks of Fire, Explosion, Self-Ignition, Lightning, Salvage, Theft, Robbery or Pilferage as below; and against any damage to the Motor and/or Car and its Equipment on board while in the hands of Transportation Companies, if caused by Stranding, Sinking, Collision, Fire, Lightning, or Derailment of any conveyance by Land or Water.

Detached Limousine or detached tops and other detached equipment belonging to the car insured hereunder are included under this policy only in such proportion as the value of such articles bears to the total value of the car insured hereunder including all such detached articles.

In the event of claim for loss or injury to Machinery, Underwriters only to be liable for cost of repairing or replacing the parts lost or injured and all charges incidental thereto.

Loss of, or damage to Motor and/or Car and its equipment whilst contained in or on the Car, or from within the building in which the Car is regularly kept, or elsewhere, by Theft, Robbery or Pilferage by persons not in the employment, service or household of the assured is covered in the event of such loss or damage being equal to or in excess of Twenty five Dollars ($25.00).

In the event of loss hereunder this Policy shall be reduced by the amount of such loss until repairs have been completed, but shall then attach for the full amount as originally written without additional premium.

The right of the assured to recover under this insurance shall not be prejudiced by any release from liability which they may give to Railroad or Transportation Companies, and the Underwriters concede to the assured the right to give such release when desired; but when the assured have not given any release, any benefits to which the assured are entitled by way of subrogation or otherwise against carriers or others shall be subrogated to the upon payment of the claim in proportion to the liability assumed by each Underwriter under contract is mutually understood and agreed that wherever in this contract or riders attaching the there reference to the hour of day, including the designation of the word "Noon" as the time when this insurance begins and terminates, such shall be construed as meaning standard time at the place where the property insured hereunder is located.

In the event of disagreement as to the amount of loss the same shall be ascertained by two competent and disinterested appraisers, the assured and A. F. Shaw & Company each selecting one, and the two so chosen shall first select a competent and disinterested umpire; the appraisers together then estimate and appraise the loss stating separately sound value and damage, and, failing to agree, shall submit their differences to the umpire; and the award in writing of any two shall determine the amount of such loss; the parties thereto shall pay the appraiser respectively selected by them and shall bear equally the expenses of the appraisal and umpire.

In the event of any claim being made hereunder the assured shall give as quickly as possible written notice thereof, together with the fullest particulars possible to A. F. SHAW & COMPANY, 159, La SALLE STREET, CHICAGO, ILLINOIS, U.S.A.

In considering the amount insured and Premium on this Policy, Five Dollars ($5.00) shall be equivalent to One Pound sterling. Loss, if any, to be payable in New York in United States currency.

during the period commencing with noon on the 24th day of March 190 7 , and ending with noon on the 24th day of March 190 8 ,

Now know Ye, that we the Insurers do hereby bind ourselves, each of his own Part and not One for Another, our Heirs, Executors, and Administrators, to make good to the Assured or to the Assured's Executors, Administrators, and Assigns, all such Loss as above stated, not exceeding the Sum of

Twenty Five Hundred Dollars

in all, that the Assured may sustain during the said period, within Thirty Days after such Loss is proved, and that in the proportions by each of Us subscribed against our respective Names.

In Witness whereof We have subscribed our Names and Proportions by us Assured.

Chicago

Dated in ~~London~~, the 24th day of March 190 7

(vertical text left margin) This Policy is not valid unless countersigned by Messrs A. F. SHAW & COMPANY, o CHICAGO, who are also authorised to initial endorsements hereon on behalf of the Underwriters.

VOID

500

George

The first American Motor Policy for $2,500 was written by the Heath syndicate was 'the branch-house floater', which gave cover of up to $\frac{1}{4}$ million on any one loss in the 700 branch-houses to which the meatyards sent their products for distribution to the butchers.

It was an age of experiment in insurance, and often the increasingly close link with the Chicago brokers led to new and esoteric methods. In 1907 one of the largest meatyards, Swifts', had formed an insurance company of their own called the Interstate Insurance Exchange. An early fore-runner of the 'captive' insurance companies by which large industrial companies nowadays use self-insurance as a means of saving premiums, it depended heavily on the conventional markets for reinsurances. At first, these had been placed in America, but now they came to the Heath syndicate through Rollins Burdick Hunter. When the Interstate was liquidated for tax reasons in 1912, its book of business was taken over by the Chicago brokers, and the reinsurances continued to be written at Lloyd's, with Cuthbert Heath as leader.

But perhaps the most important link being forged was the firm sense of trust between the American broker and client and the London underwriter. This was exemplified when Heath devised a policy to cover what were known as the 'fire divisions' in Swifts' meatyards. Rollins Burdick Hunter had been among the first brokers to set up its own department of fire engineering, and their experts now planned a scheme to break down the vast territories of the meatyards into twenty-seven divisions or compartments. Each of these could be shut off from each other by a system of doors and parapets which effectively meant that a fire in one division would not spread to others. Heath wrote the policy with a limit of $\frac{1}{4}$ million for each fire division – but what was particularly noteworthy about the policy was that it was left to the assured to decide what were the actual areas of the various fire divisions. Thus, explains Mr Adrian Palmer, the Chicago brokers' present chairman,

> after a big fire it would be left to the assured's risk manager to say whether it had been involved in four or five divisions. Conceivably there could have been a loss of $10m even in those days, but Mr Rollins always used to say the business was based on trust, and that a good risk related to good management.

Another landmark came in 1909, when the firm of C. E. Heath and Company was officially registered as a limited liability company. A company had existed before that date for according to its Memorandum of Association, the new one's first object was to:

> acquire and take over the business of insurance brokers and insurance agents carried on by Cuthbert Eden Heath, George Heath and Arthur Burns under the style of C. E. Heath and Co. Ltd. at 322 Winchester

House and at Lloyd's, and the business of underwriting carried on by the said Cuthbert Eden Heath in the same places.

Probably the move resulted from the 1908 Companies Consolidation Act, whose outstanding feature was the introduction of the private company. Under the reform such companies would not be required to file balance sheets with their annual returns because, since they did not appeal to the public for subscriptions, there was held to be no need for them to publish their private assets. Obviously it would have been of considerable advantage to Cuthbert Heath and his partners to have the limitation of liability without the necessity for disclosure.

The same year saw another new departure. For many years there had been an organization known as Lloyd's Underwriters' Association. It dealt only with marine affairs, but the word was not considered necessary in the title, for in its early days it would never have occurred to anyone that Lloyd's underwriters could possibly be concerned with other classes. When, in 1910, Cuthbert Heath and a few others formed Lloyd's Non-Marine Underwriters' Association – known as the NMA – it was a sign of a new equality within the market.

The first meeting of the new association was held in the library at Lloyd's on 5 May. A. L. Sturge – he was later to fall out with Cuthbert in the famous row over credit insurance – was elected chairman. Cuthbert Heath was one of seven committee members. The minutes of the early meetings are themselves evidence of the range of business being written in the Room, from riots and civil commotion in Mexico to conflagration hazards in the Chicago stockyards – an area where Heaths, as we have seen, were now acknowledged leaders.

Not all the risks were on such a large scale. One early NMA committee found itself considering an advertisement for dog insurance which a member of the committee had spotted on a railway station. Put up by the Katz Patent Dog Collar and Assurance Co. of Sackville Street, Piccadilly, it guaranteed the 'restoration of every lost or stolen dog having our identification marks, and we pay its value in cash which is guaranteed by Lloyd's.'

Whether or not the Katz company's boast turned out to be solidly-based we do not know, for the committee turned to other matters. One was a difficulty about insuring against the cancellation of King George V's Coronation. Under the new Insurance Act, Lloyd's underwriters, unless they had paid a special deposit, were precluded from writing cover where the death of an individual was involved, and the King's death appeared at least a possible cause of such a cancellation. Another problem discussed in 1913 has an ominously modern ring. Risks of Civil Commotion and Riots in Belfast, the committee thought, should be subject to special clauses.

Sometimes the committee found itself having to deal with public relations. Ever since Heaths' first burglary insurance, the new range of non-marine risks had been the subject of interested comment in the national press. It was a form of advertisement the NMA evidently found unwelcome: when there was a newspaper story about the insuring of a Rembrandt picture, they somewhat condescendingly discussed 'the information that finds its way into the newspapers as to insurances of a nondescript character' and decided to find some means of checking 'the indiscriminate supply of such information'.

Heath himself attended the NMA meetings irregularly. When he did so it was usually in the role of expert adviser, especially on matters of foreign insurance law. One problem he explained at length was the new legislation in New York and Illinois, which – designed as it was to protect the domestic companies – for a time seemed likely to exclude Lloyd's.

There were problems too in Norway, and one senses a feeling of awe among the committee at one meeting when 'Mr Heath suggested that as he would be seeing the Norwegian Foreign Minister in Norway in the course of the summer he proposed . . . to sound him out as to the difficulty being got over by the committee of Lloyd's placing a deposit in Norway as English insurance companies do when represented in that country.' The rest of the NMA committee were not unsophisticated men, but they were hardly used to hobnobbing with foreign ministers. The courteous giant with his deaf-aid and well-placed connections must sometimes have seemed like a being from another planet.

Indeed a certain disdain for the humdrum and the bureaucratic was an essential part of Cuthbert. Many years later a chairman of Lloyd's was to describe him as having 'a fine disregard for the conventions', and in his earlier years his rebellious streak led to continuing clashes with the committee – particularly over his practice of writing for the Excess Company from his box at Lloyd's. In 1909 he was told by the chairman, Sir John Luscombe, that there had been objections to the fact that the Excess had been accepted as a guarantor of George Heath and Cuthbert himself as underwriting names. Clearly Cuthbert regarded this somewhat technical objection as veiling a sharper one, for he wrote, in the course of a seven-page letter to Luscombe, that he could not help feeling that those who had raised the question 'really meant to imply that I was doing something to the detriment of the Room and something which I am debarred by the rules from doing.' Until a few months previously, he added, he had not read the rules which prohibited members from writing at Lloyd's for the interest of an outside company. Possibly the fact was that he knew the contents of the rules well enough to make sure he did not read them.

Having brushed the point aside at least to his own satisfaction, he went on to contend that the Excess had 'all along been a gatherer of profits for underwriters without in any way being paid for it.' It would be absurd to say, he added, that the Excess had never made anything out of Lloyd's, and it hoped to do so again. 'But I do say that Lloyd's has made far more out of the Excess,' he declared.

Few letters between Cuthbert Heath and the committee of Lloyd's have come down to us but of those that have, it is this one that above all shows his vein of crackling indignation. In it, Cuthbert also asked the chairman:

> What about the other side of the account, how much has the Excess deprived the Room of? I will tell you. For the year 1907 – *Nothing*. For the year 1908 – *Nothing*. For the year 1909 – I cannot say, but very likely *Nothing*. It only remains for me to say that should the committee virtually decide to place impediments in the way of this office account of mine, I think at least that the Room as a whole should first be consulted, and for this reason. I could not in justice to myself continue to exert myself to bring these large profits into the Room. I should be forced to accept offers, which are continually made to me, to ally the Excess with the Companies – and those the best of Companies. ... No one could reasonably expect me to refuse advantageous offers if Lloyd's, as far as the Excess is concerned, plainly intimates that it would wish to shut me out.
>
> Whether therefore the Room should be deprived of an ally which the figures prove has done much for it, is I submit a question for the Room.

Sir John Luscombe's answer has unfortunately not survived. Certainly the committee of Lloyd's was not accustomed to being answered back in quite this trenchant style, and for the time being they seem to have retreated. Then, in 1911, they summoned up courage to take action. Cuthbert was told that the practice of writing for the Excess in the Room must stop, and his response was characteristic. On receiving the committee's decree he went round to the south-east corner of the Royal Exchange, where there was a small umbrella-shop owned by a man named Carter. Heath offered to buy the lease on Carter's terms – he is said to have turned down Cuthbert's first offer of £20,000 – provided he could have immediate possession.

What the final purchase price was we do not know, but when the shop opened next morning it no longer sold umbrellas. It was the

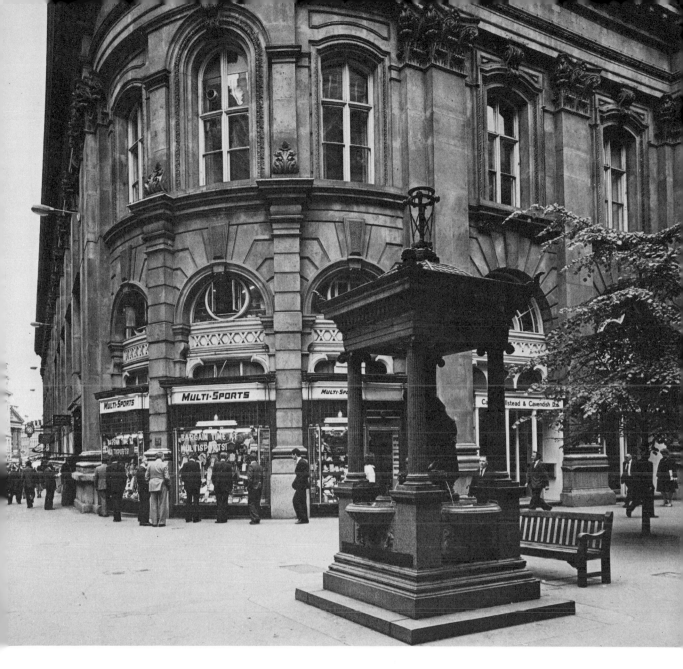

first underwriting room of the Excess – presided over by Heath, who sat there writing risks himself till the new venture was established.

Meanwhile the business of C. E. Heath and Co. was expanding to the point where Winchester House was becoming inadequate to house it. In 1912 Cuthbert launched out by taking office space in the newly-completed building opposite the Royal Exchange, known as 3–4 Royal Exchange Buildings. As one of the City's newest buildings, literally a stone's throw from Lloyd's entrance to the Royal Exchange, it must have been an impressive status

The Royal Exchange Buildings from Cornhill. The famous umbrella shop which later became the Excess Company's first office, stood on the site of what is now the sports shop

The interior of Lloyd's in 1912 with the Caller on the right

symbol to have office space there. The building still stands, separated from the Royal Exchange by the broad alley which contains Reuter's statue and two of the City's most boulevard-like lime trees.

Here the office staff would sit working at their high stools from nine till six, wearing the dark suits obligatory in those days in the City. The high stools were probably not as rigorous as they sound, for Lewis Angel, who joined Heaths in 1916, remembers them as 'in my experience one of the most comfortable ways of working since, when tired of sitting, one could stand and still see the work at eye level'. The staff, he remembers, numbered in those days about a hundred, including a few girls who had come in to replace men who had joined the army. Not only dark suits but hard hats were statutory: Angel himself bought a trilby to celebrate his first appearance at the office, and was firmly told to replace it with a bowler. His salary as a clerk was £20 a year, plus quarterly bonuses of £5 and an additional one, dependent on the profits, which could rise to £15. If Heaths' salaries were low, the office atmosphere seems to have been appealing to young people: Bruce Miller remembers being offered £60 a year by the Royal Exchange company in 1918, as against £50 at Heads and £35 at Heaths, which he eventually accepted, because of the friendly feeling he sensed there.

Cuthbert Heath himself spent most of his time in the office, now

LEFT The female staff of
Heaths in 1916. The
1914–18 War saw the
first employment of
girls in the City

BELOW Montague
Evans, Cuthbert
Heath's deputy
underwriter

going to the box comparatively rarely. His place there was usually
taken by his deputy underwriter, Montague Evans. Though pro-
fessionally a good deal more cautious than Cuthbert Heath when
it came to writing risks, Evans seems to have been what his
generation admiringly called a gay blade: he owned racehorses,
and he had a reputation as a lover of champagne and a raconteur
of risqué stories. A time-honoured anecdote tells of Evans seeking
to tell one of them to Heath, who knew his style. Heath was re-
luctant to listen at first, but consented on being told it was 'a
drawing-room story'. Cuthbert heard him out, then shook his head.
'Your drawing-room, Monty, not mine,' he told him sadly.

Another notable figure of the time could hardly have been more
different. Arthur Burns had joined the firm as manager in 1899,
and risen to great responsibility in the office. He was an ardent
Nonconformist – an embodiment of the principles Cuthbert Heath
had learnt to admire in his early days at Heads. Indeed it is said that
what first drew Cuthbert's notice to Burns was the fact that he
wore a blue temperance ribbon in his buttonhole – an act which
must have required considerable courage in the City.

Burns himself used to say that when Heath first engaged him he
forgot to fix his salary. When Burns asked a week or so later how
much he was to be paid, he was told that as office manager he should

fix the rate himself. It was the beginning of a profound and well-
placed trust between the two men. For almost forty years, he
remained Heath's most devoted servant. To the junior staff,
however, he remained a formidable figure. In 1916, recalls Lewis
Angel, 'Arthur Burns' principal job seemed to be reading through
the outgoing letters daily, looking for split infinitives and calling
the offender in for a lecture'. Burns could be caustic, too, about
commercial jargon. Any junior who began a letter with the phrase
'We beg to inform you' would be sternly told that 'Heath and Co.
don't beg. Neither do we regret and have pleasure in the same
sentence.'

In 1911 Lloyd's came under fire from a new quarter – the weekly
magazine *Truth*, which in the late summer and autumn published
a series of articles on what it called 'The Threatened Scandal at
Lloyd's'. On 9 August, *Truth* hinted darkly at impending insolvencies, especially, or so it claimed, in the non-marine market.

> If the underwriters at Lloyd's had confined themselves to marine insur-
> ance they could probably have prospered; but they were tempted to
> enter other fields in which the conditions were different from those of
> marine insurance, and are such that no prudent business man can, if he
> thinks of it, deem it wise to entrust his interests to Lloyd's ... Some
> underwriters have already found their way to the Bankruptcy Court:
> others, in big batches, will figure in the Law Courts or the Bankruptcy
> Court in the near future.

Three months later there had been no sign of a single underwriter appearing in the Law Courts, let alone 'big batches'. But
Truth was undeterred. On 4 October it came up with a report from
the *New York Journal of Commerce* which had told its readers of a

> plan to launch a Lloyd's in New York City having a large number of
> Lloyd's underwriters as the underwriting members ... The scheme con-
> templates about 200 names, the Lloyd's syndicates signed for by C. E.
> Heath being prominently named in connection with the plan.

This was the same C. E. Heath, *Truth* told its readers with mali-
cious pleasure, who 'was closely connected with an absurd system
of betting about the weather, under the title of "Pluvius" policies.'

The *Truth* arguments were to be shot down by the more powerful
guns of the *Economist* and the *Insurance and Financial Gazette* –
which on 1 November described one of them as 'the veriest piffle
we have ever seen appearing in any journal supposed to know what
it is writing about.' But there seems to have been some substance
in one thing – the suggestion that a Lloyd's syndicate might be
set up in New York. Since 1892 there had been a number of so-called

'Lloyd's' syndicates in America who had written business on the London pattern, and Heath may have thought it would be good to try to establish a legitimate Lloyd's presence in New York.

There was also a more pressing reason. This was the fact that strict new insurance laws were being imposed by the state legislature of New York. Early in 1912, in fact, Heath was to propose to the committee of Lloyd's precisely this idea of a New York syndicate as a solution to the problem. Eventually it was solved in other ways, but the facts suggest that the *New York Journal of Commerce* report, at least, was not unfounded.

This aspect apart, there can be little doubt that the *Truth* articles were indeed 'the veriest piffle'. Did the attacks on the non-marine market – and later the more specific one on Heath himself – originate from some perhaps jealous source in Lloyd's? The achievement of eminence makes any man a larger target, and Heath's was the only name which the author of the articles could reckon would be known to the outside public.

But if the mocking mention of him was any kind of attempt to damage his prestige in the market, it failed dismally. Within weeks of the *Truth* attacks, Heath received the highest accolade his market colleagues could have given him.

The occasion of it was the annual elections to the committee when three new members were chosen, each to serve four years. In December 1911 there was special interest in the elections, for the idea had been widely canvassed that there should be a stronger representation of brokers, not only of underwriters, on the committee. Among the candidates was Cuthbert Heath, who stood as a representative of both sides of the market.

Though the poll on 13 December was not declared till early evening, a large number of members stayed in the Room to hear the declaration. When it came through at six o'clock they heard that Heath had topped the poll. It was a just token of gratitude to the man who had twice come to Lloyd's rescue at a time of crisis, once by his invention of non-marine insurance, then by his introduction of the audit. Mr Heath, *The Times* informed its readers next day,

> is head of C. E. Heath and Co., brokers and underwriters, and a director of the Excess Insurance Company, the Fine Art and General Insurance Company, and of John Broadwood and Sons. He was the pioneer of Lloyd's fire business, and practically all the miscellaneous classes of insurance, the development of which was one of the causes of the introduction of Lloyd's Bill of last year. While he has been a leader in what may be described as the more hazardous risks, he has consistently pressed for safeguarding further the financial security of Lloyd's members.

Department heads at Heaths in 1910 pose for a photograph in the gardens of Brooklands, the home of George Heath (*second left*)

Heath must have felt he had his revenge on *Truth*. *The Times*, whose opinion mattered a good deal more, had put the record straight and done him justice. So had his colleagues in the Room at Lloyd's, where he was now acknowledged beyond doubt as the market's dominating figure.

The Heaths' home life at this time had an almost Arcadian quality. At Portman Square, admirals, diplomats and society beauties joined the social whirl so much beloved by Sarah. Cuthbert was an accomplished dancer: he felt the rhythm through his feet, he told his granddaughter. Altogether it was the last flare of privileged pre-war England, a golden age when, Genesta Heath remembers, 'the sun always seemed to shine in the park and there were always parasols.' King Edward's mistress, Mrs Keppel, was a neighbour, and in another house across the square lived the Countess of Warwick, that most surprising of early Socialists, and another royal mistress. The Heath children used to watch her emerging from the house at dusk alone and, they thought, 'slightly furtively.'

Nor were things much more modest at Anstie Grange, where the Heaths had moved after Sir Leopold's death in 1907. Indeed with a staff of fifty servants, if you counted grooms and ostlers, gardeners and footmen, weekend entertaining must have seemed almost an obligation. Here too, the guest-list would be composed of people from the glittering social world of London, as well as relatives and neighbours who included the Broadwoods, the Gore Brownes, and the Vaughan Williams family from Leith Hill. In those days a businessman's office and his home were worlds apart. Only three of Cuthbert's City friends ever came to Anstie – his close friend Christopher Head, Sir Raymond Beck and Eric Irgens, who was the son of the Norwegian ambassador and the firm's specialist on Scandinavian business. (Perhaps as a consequence of her French blood, Sarah seems to have always had a special penchant for foreigners: much later, in the 1920s, the guests at Anstie were irreverently known to her grandchildren as 'granny's Foreign Legion'.)

But it would be unfair to dismiss Sarah as a social butterfly. She was a shrewd, intelligent woman who found talk of politics as interesting as she probably found insurance boring. A vivid picture of a lunch-party at Anstie comes from Philip Heath, Cuthbert's second cousin, describing a visit there in 1910, when he was fifteen:

> From my point of view the lunch was a depressing affair. Cuthbert sat at one end of the table; throughout the meal he never spoke and no one paid any attention to him; the children kept quiet, and the conversation was monopolised by Sarah who never stopped talking. A conference of ambassadors was being held in London, and on the day before our visit Sarah had given a garden party in honour of the ambassadors and she hadn't got over it yet. On and on she went about the charming Count So and So, that good-looking Baron von This, the lovely Princess Some-body Else. She made me feel like a poor relation (which I was) and I reflected that this was no place for me and that I should be having my lunch with the cook and the maids in the Servants' Hall.
>
> Lunch over, Cuthbert said to Father 'Come and smoke a cigar in the study, George,' and turning to me, 'You come too, Philip.' For the rest of the afternoon he talked to me, for Father could not hear much anyway.

After a lapse of sixty-five years I remember little of what he said, except that he was explaining what a fine profession insurance was and how it should be conducted.

Perhaps the schoolboy impression of Sarah Heath was a shade unfair, but what Philip Heath remembered to the end of his days was his second cousin's kindness:

This millionaire, at the top of his profession, had devoted a whole afternoon to explaining to me, a callow schoolboy, the merits of the great profession which he clearly hoped I would enter. He had treated me as an intelligent young man and not as a schoolboy . . . until he died, I felt a deep affection for him.

The truth was that Cuthbert's and Sarah's was a very happy marriage of opposites. For Sarah, Anstie was a background to a glittering world of party-giving. For Cuthbert the beloved acres of his childhood meant a graver music. He was a devoted walker, and would disappear for hours whenever he found anyone to walk with. At other times he would stroll out with his water-colours to paint, or make endless tours of the garden with Mr Philpott, the head gardener, planning new features or exchanging the classical names of rhododendrons, so that it became a family joke that 'Father and Philpott were talking Latin.' Rhododendrons flourish to this day in the acid, peaty soil of Kitlands and Anstie. They include many rare specimens brought by Sir Leopold from his time on the Bombay station, and others grown by Cuthbert. One of his most famous specimens is still known as 'Mrs Cuthbert Heath' – a compliment which Sarah seems to have taken a little coolly. According to one story, when he rushed indoors to tell her that he had grown a new and glorious bloom and proposed calling it after her, Sarah's somewhat imperious answer was 'You'll do nothing of the kind until I've seen it.'

Partly his deafness made him more at ease in conversation with a single person, but in his deeper nature too he was diffident, a little austere and shy unless he was confident that whoever he was talking to was interested in his subject. He was not a man to let his emotions show but they were unmistakably there: when Christopher Head was lost in the *Titanic* in 1912, Genesta Heath remembers, her father heard the news in London. 'I went into the room to greet him as usual and saw something was wrong. Mother shook her head at me, to tell me to go away. He was devastated by the loss of his oldest friend.'

When she was older he would often talk to his beloved Genesta about the world of insurance. But earlier, especially as far as his family and Anstie friends were concerned, it seems to have been

Sketch of Sarah Heath by Henry Stock in her commonplace book

H.d.S.
1904
Henry Stock, the
artist

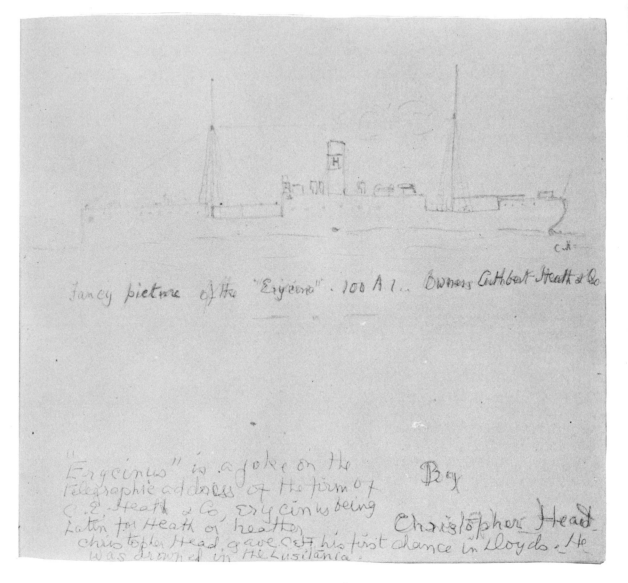

Fancy picture of the "Erycinus". 100 A 1.. Owners Cuthbert Heath & Co

"Erycinus" is a joke on the telegraphic address of the firm of C. E. Heath & Co, Erycinus being Latin for Heath or heather. Christopher Head gave C.E.H his first chance in Lloyds. He was drowned in the Lusitania.

By Christopher Head

Heath's closest friend, Christopher Head, drew this boat in Sarah's commonplace book. The name *Erycinus* – signifying 'heath' – survives as C. E. Heath's telegraphic address

something he hardly mentioned. When his cousin George asked him to contribute a note of his career to date for the Heath family records being assembled in 1912, he summed it up as follows:

His life has been the usual one of a man of business, varied and helped by the good fortune of having initiated several new features in insurance which have since developed not only in England, but in foreign insurance circles.

As a summary of the career of Cuthbert Heath till 1912, it was almost ludicrously modest.

The fact was that, at home and in the City, Cuthbert was two different people. His family knew him as shy and diffident. 'I know that he had the greatest difficulty in rebuking anyone and I believe my grandmother had to do the sacking,' recalls Mrs Joan Sarll, his granddaughter. It was the other side of the powerful figure who had flung down the gauntlet to the committee on the audit and was to do so again on the issue of credit insurance. In the nature of the courteous giant, the steel was never far below the surface.

No story of insurance is complete without its anecdotes of fraud and theft. One of the most intriguing is that of the Great Pearl Robbery in 1913, a *cause célèbre* which involved the largest loss so far on a jewellery policy at Lloyd's.

The client in the case was one Max Mayer, a leading Hatton Garden dealer. He had a policy, led by the Heath syndicate, which covered his stock for all risks anywhere in Europe. Part of this stock was a famous necklace: consisting of sixty-one graduated pearls, it had been offered for sale for £150,000 to a Paris dealer.

The Paris dealer had returned it by post, and one day in July 1913 the package arrived at Mayer's office – apparently intact with its seals unbroken. When he opened it, however, the contents turned out to be eleven lumps of sugar and a screwed-up bit of a Paris newspaper.

A special committee of Lloyd's underwriters was set up to handle the affair, headed by Montague Evans. Weeks passed with no news of the necklace, and then another Paris dealer named Brandstatter came up with a piece of news. On a visit to Antwerp, he told the underwriters, he had been approached and asked to bid for a necklace which looked like Mr Mayer's.

The underwriters, acting with the police, began to lay their plans. M. Brandstatter and two other dealers – one of them the underwriters' agent – were to meet the suspected thieves at a hotel in Holborn, where the police would be lying in wait in order to arrest them. But the criminals – now known to be headed by a noted jewel-thief named Cammi Grizzard – must have got wind of what was going to happen. The meeting between the dealers and the thieves took place, but there was no sign of Grizzard or the necklace.

But neither the police nor the underwriters had any intention of giving up. Another meeting was arranged, this time at Chancery Lane tube station. Grizzard turned up and was arrested – but still there was no necklace.

Two weeks later a workman was walking along the Caledonian Road and saw a matchbox in the gutter. He picked it up, opened it, and found it contained what he thought was a cheap imitation necklace. He showed it to some friends in a pub, who told him to take it to the police. He did so, and when the police examined it, they found it was Max Mayer's missing necklace.

When the thieves were put on trial the facts became a little clearer. The Mayer necklace had been returned from Paris, but on the way to Mayer's, the postman had called at the shop of another dealer whose name was Silverman. While he was in Silverman's shop the package had been opened, the necklace removed, and the envelope resealed.

The prisoners were found guilty and sentenced, but the case still begged some questions. How had someone at Silverman's shop managed to extract the necklace and reseal the package without the postman knowing? Why, if the theft had taken place in London, was a piece of a French newspaper put in among the lumps of sugar? And why had someone else dropped a necklace worth £150,000 in a Caledonian Road gutter?

Probably the riddle will never be solved, but the case did no harm to underwriters. The world of insurance has a way of turning claims to good account, and the public interest aroused by the case brought a huge demand for jewellers' all-risks insurance. Perhaps the best summing-up of the whole affair is that of Mr Percy Holford, who later became Heaths' jewellery underwriter: 'A wonderful advertisement for our business.'

Meanwhile Cuthbert Heath's election to the committee had brought him not merely a prestigious status. As a new member he was an assiduous attender at the meetings: he also seems to have become, as he had been on a smaller scale at the NMA, a kind of foreign minister for the market. Almost immediately after his election we find him briefing the committee on the problems of New York and Illinois where, he told them, 'new and drastic regulations' demanded that agents be appointed and policy forms filed. His own solution to the problem was both interesting and prophetic: since before the turn of the century, there had been several insurance syndicates trading in New York borrowing Lloyd's name. Heath's idea was that the committee of the real Lloyd's might:

> acquire an existing organisation and ... work under its name. Such an organisation has been offered to us. It is called the New York Lloyd's, and is one of the older institutions.

Nothing appears to have come of the suggestion, but if it had been acted upon, the present-day insurance scene might be very different, for in the summer of 1978 arrangements were made to set up an insurance market, similar to Lloyd's but completely independent of it, in New York. At the time of writing it is hard to guess how much of a competitive threat this may be to Lloyd's of London, but what does seem clear is that Heath's idea, had it been taken up, might have established a Lloyd's presence in New York to the incalculable advantage of the London market.

Meanwhile in 1913 the American problems rumbled on, and in the September we find Cuthbert seeing the representatives of the New York State Legislature on behalf of the committee. Norway, too, continued to present problems, and in July 1912 he had told the committee that the Norwegian government were anxious about reports that Lloyd's underwriters would not pay Norwegian claims in time of war, and that he had seen the Norwegian minister in London to discuss the matter.

It is significant of Heath's breadth and scope of mind that he was always using his influence and drive to push Lloyd's forward – sometimes a little faster than it wanted. In 1913, the committee considered a request from C. E. Heath and Co. to admit an American broker as an underwriting member. It was not the first attempt: a year or so before Cuthbert's election, the company had put forward a similar request on behalf of a French insurance man named Helbronner. The committee's response was negative and – one guesses – slightly startled. They were, Heaths were informed, 'unable to entertain the admission of people non-resident in the United Kingdom.' Heath was more than forty years ahead of his time. It was not till 1965 that Lloyd's took the revolutionary step of admitting foreign members.

Both his involvement in Lloyd's foreign affairs and his advocacy of foreign names point to another side of Cuthbert Heath. Lloyd's, on the one hand deeply conservative and very English, had always depended on its worldwide business. Julius Angerstein, who had himself reformed Lloyd's in the eighteenth century, had been a German born in St Petersburg. Nobody could have been more English than Cuthbert, but his intelligence and family background – not to mention the international nature of his business – made him far broader in his outlook than most of his colleagues. Sarah, with her Gambier blood, must have been an unconscious influence too. Perhaps there were moments when he could have wished her fleets of foreign guests back in their embassies. But they, too, in their way, were contributors to his international outlook.

Meanwhile the Arcadian time was running out. In August 1914 the world stood on the edge of risks, hazards and perils that even Lloyd's had never thought of.

One day in January 1915, what onlookers described as 'a report as if a big gun had been fired' was heard in the main street of Great

Yarmouth. People came rushing out on to the street to see what was the matter. Noises described as being 'of a terrifying kind' were heard in different parts of the town. Two Zeppelins were seen passing over Cromer – 'the size of a church' said one awestruck man at Hunstanton.

A new and horrendous era of history had begun: the age of aerial bombing. The bombs dropped on the east coast towns of Yarmouth and King's Lynn that January day killed a boy, an old lady, a middle-aged shoemaker, and a soldier's widow. They also partly demolished several houses and smashed, said one report, 'a thousand windows'.

Almost at once there was a rush of householders and business-men to insure their property, but the immediate reaction from the companies was predictably conservative and cautious. There was no data on which to assess rates, the fire offices said, and nor did they think it proper to jeopardise funds set aside for holders of conventional fire-policies.

Once again it was left to Lloyd's to make the running. From the beginning of the war there had been fears of air-raids, and business firms in particular had come to Lloyd's for insurance against the Zeppelins. Though the first air-raid cover seems to have been written by Sidney Boulton – Cuthbert's old ally in the audit battle – Heath himself had, since 1914, been writing a Householder's Compre-hensive policy which covered damage caused by 'aeroplanes, airships and or other aerial craft', as well as by 'riots, strikes and suffragists'. Soon he had also become the leader on specific in-surances against air-bombing. 'It was not very difficult,' he was later to write,

> to arrive at a premium in spite of the apparent uncertainty. We knew roughly how many airships Germany possessed, or were likely to pos-sess, and we also knew roughly how many bombs they could carry and also the area of possible damage by one bomb. Taking London as the example, it was easy to ascertain what premium should be charged to cover probable risks. I remember being very much surprised when I dis-covered how much of London is represented by open spaces. In the end I multiplied the probable hazard by six and thought I should be on the right side.

By early 1915 the rate was still the original one of 2s. for every £100 of cover, 'though the rates would stiffen,' recalls George Thomson, 'after a heavy dose of bombing.' Thomson had joined Heaths in 1914, through Arthur Burns' acquaintance with his father, a Nonconformist minister in Yorkshire. One of his first jobs on the box, he recalls, was to update the syndicate's book

George Thomson who
was Chairman of
Lloyd's in 1961

containing records of its risks 'in any given area from Brighton to
Sheerness'. Often he would sit at the box till seven o'clock in the
evening, entering the details of the day's raids. Sometimes the
reality behind the account books came uncomfortably close: 'I
remember coming out of the Royal Exchange on a winter evening
and seeing a Zeppelin going its ponderous way, caught in the criss-
cross of the searchlights.' Soon he and the rest of the young men
on the box were to exchange their quills for rifles, and their city
suits for khaki.

ABOVE German Naval Airship L.53. Cuthbert Heath was the first underwriter to insure against death or damage to property by Zeppelins during the First World War

OPPOSITE Bomb damage in the Minories in the 1914–18 War. The bomb has fallen almost immediately opposite the site of C. E. Heath & Co's present building

Heath's pre-eminence in air-raid insurance was recognised when he was asked to serve on the five-man committee headed by the Rt. Hon. F. Huth Jackson, which the government had called on to draw up a scheme of air-raid insurance. The committee must have worked fast, for the scheme came into effect in July 1915. The rates remained those proposed by Sidney Boulton – 2s. per cent for private houses and 3s. for other buildings, with a rate of 7s. 6d. per cent on merchandise in the docks. Policies included damage from anti-aircraft shells as well as bombs, while people in east coast areas, which were vulnerable to the further hazard of bombardment from the sea, could get additional cover for the risk for an extra shilling, or 1s. 6d. for industrial buildings.

When the scheme was revised in 1917 premium rates were halved, a step which *The Times* assumed to be

justified by a very considerable balance in hand on account of this business. Certainly aircraft insurance is believed to have been very profitable to those underwriters who met the demand for insurance before the Government scheme came into operation. Ever since the Government scheme was inaugurated in the summer of 1915 a very large amount of aircraft insurance has been placed in the open market, especially in connexion with risks not included in the Government scheme, such as loss of profits.

Loss of profits had been one of Cuthbert Heath's first inventions. Now, coupled with the air bombing cover, it was a formidable example of the tight cocoon of cover spun by his innovations.

There is an endearing glimpse of Cuthbert Heath around this time in the memoirs of a famous Frenchman. In 1913, Edouard Herriot, later to be Prime Minister of France, was Mayor of Lyons and planning the great exhibition to be held there in 1914. In order to insure it against a possible deficit, he travelled to London over the New Year holiday. He made his way to Lloyd's, where he was introduced to Cuthbert.

Heath's immediate reaction to the idea of insuring the Lyons exhibition seems to have been amusement. Every time anyone asked him to insure an exhibition, he told Herriot, they promised a brilliant success and exceptional profits but in the event, things always turned out so that he had to face a deficit.

'However, that's of no importance. Here is a pencil and a slip of paper. Write down the amount for which you wish to be guaranteed. I will deduct the premium to be paid, and the deal will be closed.'

M. Herriot asked for a guarantee of three million francs, and promised to pay a premium of a quarter of a million. To his astonishment 'the whole thing was drawn up in a single sentence – and written with a lead pencil.'

Evidently this informal way of doing business baffled M. Herriot. Where, he asked Heath, would they go to find a lawyer to transform their contract into a legal document?

Heath laughed. 'Will a lawyer be more honest than we are? Put your slip of paper in your pocket and when you get home put it in your safe deposit box. And sleep well.'

Thus ended M. Herriot's first encounter with Lloyd's underwriters. He returned to France, worked on his exhibition which – the outbreak of war intervening – opened late and was greeted, he wrote, with every sort of hazard.

> A tempest soaked the buildings; a sudden rising of the Rhône carried away the bridge that led to the fairgrounds; strikes raged. What, I wondered, was to become of me? Full of anxiety, I wrote in the autumn to the good Mr Heath.

Heath replied at once. He was unable to do anything at the moment because he was heavily engaged with writing the new Zeppelin insurance. Could M. Herriot wait a few days longer?

M. Herriot could, and a few days later a loss adjuster appointed by Heaths, Mr Price, arrived in Lyons. He rapidly verified M. Herriot's accounts, 'then, in the elegant flourish with which one

offers flowers to a lady he handed me the cheque which freed me.'

Early next morning Mr Price set off for London – just before the City Treasurer of Lyons found that in reckoning the exchange rate, Price had miscalculated. He had overpaid M. Herriot by 25,000 francs. As soon as the mistake was found M. Herriot cabled Cuthbert Heath. The response was characteristic. 'Give the money to a French war charity.'

'Now I knew what an English signature meant,' was the future Prime Minister's final comment.

The episode of the Lyons exhibition was only one example of the generous style that informed Heath's underwriting. During the war a client insured himself against being killed on a trip to the United States, at the time of the U-boat menace. The ship escaped the U-boats, but on his trip to America the man caught a fever from which he died. His widow claimed on the insurance policy but Heath for once refused to pay: for the sake of other insurers, he felt, it was wrong that someone should be able to claim on a risk

Lyons around the time of the 1913 Exhibition which was insured by Cuthbert Heath where they had not in fact been covered. The widow took the case to court and lost. Cuthbert then gave her the whole amount she had claimed and all her costs.

The incident was doubly characteristic. Generosity meant much to Cuthbert Heath, and so did business discipline. He insisted that justice must be done and be seen to be done – then tempered with kindness and compassion.

Though he remained on the Committee of Lloyd's for the statutory four years, Heath's attendance at its meetings seems to have become gradually less frequent. Perhaps his deafness prevented him taking a full part in meetings when ten or more people were speaking. Another reason may have been his growing involvement in various forms of war-work. In 1915 he became a trustee of Lloyd's Patriotic Fund, which, dating from the Napoleonic Wars, now found itself more than ever engaged in giving assistance to soldiers and sailors in distress, or to the families of men killed in action.

In the same year he made his office available as a kind of recruiting centre. From 26 November, he told the committee at almost the last meeting he attended, two doctors and two attesting officers would be on duty to examine and swear in young Lloyd's men joining the Army Reserve under the scheme promoted by Lord Derby. 'Of course we are all thinking of the war,' he wrote to a friend in America five months earlier,

> and very little else outside our business. I have already lost one nephew and two young cousins, but even the mothers are very brave and somehow the common losses seem to make the individual ones easier to bear . . . In our neighbourhood ten per cent of the population has volunteered for the Army or Navy. My boy will be transferred to motor machine guns soon, we think, and then our own particular anxieties will begin.

Any young man setting out for the services from the Coldharbour district would be summoned to Anstie for a benevolent talk in Cuthbert's study. But it was already in his mind that, for the duration of the war, he would give up Anstie. In September 1916 he gave the house to the War Office for use as an officer's hospital. Heath fitted it out as a hospital at his own expense, giving the normal government grant to his neighbour Lady Carnavon, to help her run another hospital.

Nearly 700 patients passed through the Anstie hospital between 1916 and 1918, and were cared for by a staff of fifty. One of its most junior members was his daughter Genesta, who had been only fifteen when the war had started. In a contribution to the Heath family records she gave an account of her time as a pantry-maid which foreshadows the lively and engaging style she was later to develop as a writer:

At one time Anstie took in 63 patients, but later it was cut down to 47. We may not have been able to sing in tune, or make a chart, or dress a wound, but we certainly could wash up. We used to wash and dry from 250–300 things – plates, cups, silver, tea and coffeepots etc., in about two hours. It really takes a lot of doing . . . for you may get them clean and broken, or you may get them dirty and whole, but clean and all in one piece takes an expert pair of hands . . . Sometimes after a hard day's work – which meant that we were actually on our feet, and running about with laden trays for the eleven or twelve hours duty a day   I felt giddy and speechless with fatigue, and the thought of having to get out of bed at 6.15 next morning was nearly enough to make me curl up on the dining-room floor and sleep in all my clothes, hugging the broom that had to sweep the carpet next day! But the only time when I made a habit of that was on convoy nights.

A convoy arriving was always, to me, a very wonderful sight. The men came to us straight from the front, for Anstie was a first-line hospital. The lorries came over from Aldershot – it made a forty-five mile drive there and back, just to bring the patients from Holmwood Station to the hospital, a distance of half a mile! and they were often driven by women. Half an hour before the train arrived, grey, silent beings materialised out of thin air and turned into VTC men – stretcher bearers.

They gathered in front of the house and yawned piteously. Then a purring up the drive, then those huge headlights, and the sudden appearance of our Commandant's figure in the doorway, very tall and slim, in red uniform with the long white veil reaching below her waist. A cloak over her shoulders blurred the outline, and she carried a lantern. The ambulance came round to the door, immediately the crowd of stretcher-bearers flocked to it, and the stretchers were drawn out, 'very carefully and slow'. It was wonderfully impressive to me, and the first time I saw it I wanted to weep . . .

. . . Once I was showing a soldier visitor upstairs, and he said to me by way of conversation '*Awful* place this for a hospital, what?' I could think of nothing else to say but 'It *is* rather a long way from the station.' When I took him his tea I heard him ask his friend who I was – and he must have been surprised to find that the 'awful place' was my home.

CHAPTER FIVE

The Courteous Giant

By the time the First World War ended Cuthbert Heath was almost sixty. In one sense he was now Lloyd's most authoritative figure. Yet, as his clash with the committee over credit insurance was to show, he was still its *enfant terrible*.

The credit insurance battle of 1923 is among Lloyd's most famous sagas. But to understand its background we must go back briefly to the 1890s, when credit insurance first began to be written on the London market.

Basically the object of credit insurance is to insure a merchant or manufacturer against bad debts. In the nineteenth century the bill of exchange was the device which enabled foreign trade to flourish. If a British merchant was selling goods to, say, Peru, then his Peruvian client would give him a bill of exchange, usually payable three months later. Occasionally something would go wrong with these transactions: if so, credit insurance provided a protection for the trader. Under it, the insurer would pay the value of the bill of exchange if the foreign purchaser failed to meet his obligations.

Historically there was nothing new about credit insurance. From the earliest times Mediterranean traders had obtained guarantees against the possibility of their customers failing to pay up, but despite its long history the method had never been widely used in England. But by the later years of the nineteenth century the expansion of trade was giving the concept new importance, and in the 1890s the first significant credit insurance company, the National Provincial Trustee and Assets Corporation, came in being. Its mode of operation was, we read:

> to insure that the merchant would recover fifty percent of his loss in the event of default on the part of the acceptor of the bill. The conditions of the policy were of a somewhat voluminous character, but were not onerous, and the demand for insurances of this kind was much larger than could be dealt with by the small market that existed for placing these risks.

PREVIOUS PAGE 1928 Lagonda. Between the two world wars, motoring became increasingly popular bringing special problems to Lloyd's

Arthur Burns has left an account of how the National Provincial came to be involved with the Heath syndicate, and because the event was a landmark in what was to be one of Cuthbert's most momentous innovations, it is worth quoting in a little detail. 'The period about 1892,' Burns writes,

> was one of great financial trouble in Australia owing to bad seasons and unwise extension of bank facilities which brought down some and greatly crippled others. Owing to this trouble merchants in this country who were in the habit of shipping goods to Australia became, not unnaturally, apprehensive as to the fate that might await the bills which they were accustomed to draw on Australian houses in payment for goods shipped to them, and they looked around to see if they could secure protection against this risk.

Meanwhile the National Provincial had begun to undertake credit insurance from its offices in Queen Street. But when it began to write the Australian business, it found itself in need of reinsurance. Its manager, George Shoenfield, had tried two firms of Lloyd's brokers without success. Burns himself was then working for a Lloyd's broker named Oliverson Auckland, and in 1893 he happened to place a risk of theirs with Shoenfield who asked him – probably as a *quid pro quo* – if he could help him to place a reinsurance cover. Burns' narrative continues:

> On showing the business in the Room I came into touch with the two brokers in question, both of whom advised me not to waste time and shoe leather over it . . . Mr Heath declined the business to me, but said that if I could find someone else to lead he would follow. After some time I did secure a small lead from another underwriter and Mr Heath put his own line down. It was, of course, a very small affair, the limit being only a few hundreds on any one firm, but anyway it was a start and I believe the reinsurance premium income for the first twelve months was about £400.

The story of credit insurance might have been very different if the National Provincial had not soon afterwards found itself in trouble – not over credit insurance itself, but through other financial deals. One particularly unfortunate one, Burns notes, was in connection with the site of the Haymarket Theatre. Eventually the National Provincial ceased business altogether, and it was at this point that Lloyd's underwriters began to take an interest. Cuthbert Heath was among those who decided to see if they could salve something from it. Another was H. S. Spain, a protégé of Arthur Burns, who had met Spain at his local church in Essex.

It was in 1896, Spain recalled later, that Lloyd's underwriters first began to take an interest:

> It was a somewhat cautious group that took the plunge – for it was a plunge, and almost in the dark. Very little could be gathered in the way of statistics, and the experience of others in the business was – to say the

least – not very encouraging. To cut a long story short the underwriters were determined to make a book, and not nibble haphazardly at stray applications. A syndicate was formed under the somewhat lengthy title of the Trade Acceptance Guarantee Syndicate of Underwriting Members of Lloyd's. That syndicate consisted of only five or seven names, the chief surviving member being Mr Cuthbert Heath.

In his later years credit insurance was to become almost a hobby-horse of Cuthbert's. Indeed when he clashed with the committee of Lloyd's over it in 1923, there were those who said that it was almost an *idée fixe* with him. But in these early days none of this enthusiasm was apparent. Partly the scale of business was limited before the 1914 war. Certainly the subject seems to have claimed little of his interest at a time when his teeming insurance brain was throwing off other glittering policy ideas like sparks from a catherine-wheel.

In 1901 the new syndicate's interests were sold to the Commercial Union – but, bandied about like an unwanted child, the vicissitudes of credit insurance were still not over. Before long one of the Commercial Union directors, who was also involved in bill-discounting, decided that this might clash with his credit insurance interests. In 1903 the business was sold once more, this time to the Excess Company which Cuthbert had founded nine years earlier.

Back in the Heath fold, the progress of the business seems to have been moderate until the war, when the Board of Trade set up a committee to look into the question of financial facilities for British traders when peace came. The result of this was the creation of the British Trade Corporation, one of whose aims was 'that arrangements should be made for the insurance of commercial bills.' The Corporation's first ordinary general meeting was held at the end of January, 1918, when Lord Faringdon announced that it had decided:

> to create a separate company that would be entirely under its control for doing the class of business referred to, and it had entered into an agreement with the Excess Insurance Company to transfer to the new concern the part of the Excess Company's business of this character, and with the business they also transferred to the new undertaking their underwriter, Mr H. S. Spain, who had for many years past devoted his energies to credit insurance. It was hoped that the new undertaking would meet a genuine demand, and it should be particularly useful to the smaller trader, who was without the facilities that were possessed by the large merchant and manufacturer.

The new company – it was to be known as the Trade Indemnity Company – was only one half of the new plan for government backed credit insurance. The other half would come in 1919 with the setting-up of what was then known as the Export Credit Scheme. The precursor of the modern Export Credits Guarantee Department, this not only protected exporters from defaulting creditors but also from political and war risks. Between them the two organizations would provide a complete cocoon of security for traders and exporters.

In setting up the Trade Indemnity Company, the government had availed itself of the expertise of London's pre-eminent insurer. As for Cuthbert himself, he had always been deeply aware of the responsibility insurance owed to trade. 'The fact of the matter,' he once said,

> is that insurance is rather like a stone thrown into the water. The ripples of it go on getting wider and wider and touch more and more points as they widen. And the more points insurance touches, the more it can eliminate risks, surely the more good we shall do not only to trade, but in solving *the* great problem – that of providing equal opportunity.

The other point about Cuthbert Heath was that he was not an Admiral's son for nothing. Throughout his life he deployed his resources – companies and syndicates, insurance and reinsurance – with infinite tactical skill. Chief of these resources – and moreover the one to which he owed a special loyalty – was his Lloyd's connection. Now, as credit insurance began to spread, he not unnaturally foresaw a close involvement for the Lloyd's market with his new company's transactions.

It was a hope to be dashed, however, from an unexpected quarter.

In 1923 Lloyd's found itself faced with its most notorious scandal ever. This centred on an underwriter named Stanley Harrison who had become a member of Lloyd's in 1917. Harrison controlled both a brokerage business and an underwriting agency, and ran a syndicate which included motor business.

One of the effects of the post-war motoring boom had been the spread of companies selling cars by hire purchase. When the companies wanted to raise cash to buy more cars, they obtained it from the discount houses on the strength of bills of exchange signed by the customers already buying cars on hire purchase. But because the hire purchase companies were still something of a novelty, the discounter was not always too ready to cash these bills. But if the hire purchase company could show an insurance policy which guaranteed the credit of the purchase, the discount houses were a good deal more likely to be forthcoming.

This was the background to a large proportion of Harrison's

Lloyd's in 1927, the
year before the move
to Leadenhall Street

underwriting business. At first the hire-purchase companies had
gone for credit insurance, or guarantee policies, as they were
sometimes known, to the companies. Then they had discovered a
cheaper market at Lloyd's and begun, says Gibb, 'to favour certain
Lloyd's underwriters, of whom the busiest, the least inquisitive and
most dashing was Harrison.'

The chronicle of Harrison's disasters is too long and complex to
to concern us in detail. They stemmed from a basically slapdash
attitude to the business he was asked to write, and to the fact that
he entirely failed to distinguish between sound companies and bad
ones. Later he was to compound this by using bills of his own,
backed by his own insurance policies, even when he knew that
these were worthless.

His eventual downfall came about in a bizarre fashion. One of his clients was a man named Holsteinson, a Swede who lived in London. Holsteinson claimed that his business was running fleets of charabancs and taxis. Probably there was some truth in this, but a large part of his fleet was non-existent: as an original way of raising cash, Holsteinson had invented a string of imaginary vehicles, and then drawn bills upon them. The bills had been insured with Harrison's syndicate and then discounted. When Holsteinson chose his moment to flee the country in 1923, Harrison learnt that this particular fraud had involved him in a loss of £17,000.

Harrison might possibly have been able to raise the £17,000 had he not been beset by other troubles. Overriding all these was the fact that he had committed an almost ludicrously transparent deception on the Audit. For a year or more he had been keeping two sets of accounts. The first, designed to be shown to the Audit committee, bore no relation to the facts. The other, which he kept to himself, contained the true record of his underwriting.

Harrison spent the summer of 1923 desperately trying to write himself out of trouble. Then in October his bank refused to honour one of his cheques. Harrison was called before A. L. Sturge, the chairman. At a rough count, Sturge discovered, the syndicate's debts were at least £200,000.

What followed was one of the landmarks in Lloyd's history. Harrison had made his confession to Sturge on 3 October. Eight days later, Sturge called a meeting of all the underwriting agents in the Committee Room. If Harrison's debts were not paid in full, he told them, the name of Lloyd's would be seriously damaged 'and will never recover during our lifetime'. What he then asked was something unheard of in the market – that the combined members of Lloyd's should raise the money to pay the debts in full, each syndicate paying a share proportionate to its premium income.

Reading the verbatim account of the meeting on that October morning one can still sense the tension and anxiety of the market. But its answer was unanimous – they would pay up as Sturge had asked. Eventually the debt was found to be more than £360,000, but the underwriters kept their promise, paying shares of the debt which ranged from £10,000 to one member's eightpence.

Thus the Harrison affair came to what Sturge called 'a heroic conclusion', but there was another aspect. When the truth about his underwriting was revealed, it was not only Harrison himself who incurred the underwriters' anger. Credit insurance as a whole became a dirty word throughout the market.

With hindsight it is easy to say that both the committee and the members of Lloyd's over-reacted to the events of that October. Credit insurance, Harrison had shown, was easy to abuse. But from there the market went on to assume that the business was, as Gibb describes their feeling about it, 'too explosive to be handled'. On 7 November Sturge told the underwriting agents that in future no account would be audited that included this type of business. All policies would bear a statement that the securities and guarantees held by Lloyd's did not apply to credit insurance.

For Cuthbert Heath this decision was quite simply a disaster. His new Trade Indemnity Company was steadily writing an increasing book of business. Premium income had gone up from £12,000 in 1918 to £122,000 in 1924, but now the committee's decision would cut the ground clean away from Lloyd's involvement in its business.

Nor was it simply a matter of losing markets. Heath was a loyal Lloyd's man but he was also by now a passionate enthusiast for the new type of business. H. S. Spain, lecturing to the Corporation of Insurance Brokers the following year, said that since the war British traders had found it

> almost impossible to do a sufficient amount of trade in some countries in consequence of the war, and English firms have attempted to discover new markets in countries where before the war they had never traded. The credit company has sources of investigation which are not possessed by the merchants, and I think my company can claim to have built up a system which has been of great service to its clients.

On the complex and difficult question of trade with Russia, added Spain, brokers' enquiries were coming to him hourly.

For Heath it must have been infinitely galling to see such prospects squandered because of the misdeeds of one shady underwriter. But there was another point as well. He saw the refusal to allow credit insurance not only as contrary to Lloyd's long-cherished tradition of freedom, but as in fact illegal. The Lloyd's Non-Marine Act of 1911 had specifically stated that Lloyd's should carry on insurance of every description 'including guarantee' or credit business.

The illegality was the chink in the committee's armour, and Heath went for it remorselessly. If the Board of Trade was persuaded by Lloyd's to adopt Sturge's proposed changes in the Audit, Heath said, he was prepared to go to law to stop them doing so.

At the prospect of a court clash between Lloyd's and its most famous member, tempers frayed on both sides. A. L. Sturge was a Quaker who had been among Heath's close colleagues in the early days of the Non-Marine Association, but the two men's temperaments were very different. The clash between them was, says Gibb, 'severe and sharp', and soon they were not even speaking.

J. F. Kennedy Airport, New York, which is operated by the Port Authority of New York and New Jersey

If things had been permitted to go on like this it might have been Lloyd's itself rather than its freedom to write credit insurance which would have perished. As luck would have it, the New Year saw a change of chairman, Sturge being succeeded by E. E. Adams. The new chairman did not press the proposed changes in the audit, and a negotiator was found in the person of R. W. Roylance, the chairman of the Non-Marine Association, who later said he had worn out a pair of shoes walking between the committee room and Heath's office.

At the price of a pair of shoes, Roylance's services to the market were a bargain. By October 1924, a year after Harrison's confession, a compromise was hit on. It was the ingenious one that credit insurance could not be written directly at Lloyd's, but that it could be written in the form of reinsurance. 'Lloyd's in future would not be allowed to drink its credit insurance straight from the tap, but might drink it out of an approved filter,' comments Gibb.

For Cuthbert Heath the episode brought something as near defeat as he ever came to in the market. But his natural resilience and skill in deploying his resources quickly transformed the situation. Forbidden the involvement of Lloyd's, he turned to the companies. Early in 1924 the original arrangement with the British Trade Corporation was scrapped. The Trade Indemnity Company's capital was increased from £100,000 to £250,000 and a new board was set up, composed of the general managers of such companies as the Commercial Union, the Royal Exchange, the Prudential, the Yorkshire, the London and Lancashire and the Atlas. Cuthbert Heath remained chairman and Spain the underwriter. The Company's premium income continued to increase and, thanks to the committee's compromise, Cuthbert saw that Heaths placed its reinsurance business in the Lloyd's market.

The last word on his contribution to the story of credit insurance came in 1959, two decades after Cuthbert's death. It was spoken by Sir Frank Nixon, then head of the Export Credit Guarantee Department which was later to embody so much of Heath's thinking on the subject:

> The supremacy of the Bill of Exchange which lasted over a hundred years has been a little diminished. War, nationalism and the general feeling of insecurity have made it difficult for the Bill of Exchange in the twentieth century to fulfil the same role that it did in the nineteenth. Just as it took a genius to invent a Bill of Exchange, so it required another genius to devise and launch the instrument which might not supplant but supplement the Bill in this brave, new and insecure age. I believe that that instrument is the credit insurance policy. I believe that the genius who launched it was Cuthbert Heath.

ABOVE The Oval cricket ground. C. E. Heath & Co are insurance brokers to the Surrey County Cricket Club

BELOW Ocean-going tows are a commonplace risk in the marine insurance market today

Thomas Frost. Frost was one of the triumvirate of brokers – the others being Charles Gould and Harry Lyons – who brought a new dash of enterprise to Heaths in the 1920s

It may seem surprising that we have progressed this far with so little mention of Heaths as brokers. Essentially the reason is that in Cuthbert Heath's early days the underwriters were the mandarins of the market. The brokers in those days fulfilled the more humdrum role of suppliers of business. Nor were broking houses the giants they are today. Only a few, like Sedgwick Collins, Price Forbes, Heads, Hartley Cooper and Willis, Faber and Dumas, the marine specialists, were known outside a small circle in the City.

Now, in the post-war world, this balance of power in the market was beginning to alter. Brokers were beginning to travel further afield: when one went off in search of surplus line business from the United States, his competitors must follow, or if possible pre-empt him. A new trend was developing, especially in the key area of American non-marine, where the broker was becoming expert in every aspect of his client's business.

One firm which typified this modern expert, aggressive style was the Lloyd's broking house of Morgan Lyons, whose chairman, Henry Lyons, was the epitome of the showy virtues of the broker. Coming from what were, by Cuthbert's standards, humble beginnings – his father was one of the waiters in the Room – he was one of the first people to breach Lloyd's still hierarchic social structure. He had blazed the broking trail to America soon after the San Francisco earthquake when, according to one Heaths man, 'half the American companies were bust. You could pick up business like picking pebbles off the seashore.'

Lyons and his team of brokers, including Tommy Frost and Charles Gould – the latter especially was cast in the archetypal mould of the ebullient, optimistic broker – became almost daily attenders at the Heath box because of their speciality in American non-marine business. Lyons' exuberant style had made him a favourite with Americans, and on his travels he had built up some formidable accounts through such leading brokers as Walter Brandt, the marine and all-risks specialists in San Francisco, and Heaths' own Chicago correspondents, Rollins Burdick Hunter. Soon these contacts were to be merged, for in the early 1920s Lyons approached Cuthbert Heath with a view to selling him his business. A deal was done on the basis that Heaths would take over Morgan Lyons and run it in exchange for half the brokerage commission.

The takeover became effective from 1 January 1924. Lyons retired from active broking and turned his attention to Liberal politics, eventually becoming Lord Ennisdale and devoting himself to the keeping of polo ponies, which he sometimes lent to the Prince of Wales. Both Frost and Gould were to leave a permanent mark on Heaths' broking style. Frost was later to bring the company

Charles Gould, one of
Heath's team of
brokers who
specialized in
American non-marine
business

many major clients, while Gould, as chairman of Heaths in the
mid-1950s, was to preside over a period of major changes. More
generally, the takeover resulted in a large increase in Heaths'
broking connection, with no equivalent rise in overheads. From
now on, the name of C. E. Heath & Co. would come more and more
to be linked with broking.

The early 'twenties saw changes of scene both for Cuthbert and for
Heaths. After twenty years Cuthbert himself decided to move from

Portman Square to Aldford Street, just off Park Lane, where he had bought three small houses and pushed them into one. The move seems to have been not without its problems. One of the vendors stuck out for what must have been a formidable price, for the records of the Excess Company show loans of over £69,000 to Cuthbert for buildings in Aldford Street and Park Street through 1920–21. Eventually all was completed to Cuthbert's satisfaction, the only casualty of the move being his cherished Adam ceiling with its ladies in medallions and loops of flowers, which unfortunately crumbled when he made a perhaps ill-advised attempt to move it the short distance across Oxford Street from Portman Square. But if he had lost a ceiling he had gained a garden. One of its features was a fountain – which is still remembered in the name of the present building on the site, Fountain House.

The new house in Aldford Street was, Genesta Heath recalls, 'a hundred per cent more comfortable' than Portman Square, and perhaps the added space gave Cuthbert the idea that he should also move his office to more spacious quarters. Just before Christmas 1923 Heaths crossed the street from the Royal Exchange to new premises over Waterlows, the stationers, on the corner of Cornhill and Birchin Lane. It was significant of the tight-knit nature of Cuthbert Heath's enterprise that all his early offices – Royal Exchange Buildings, Birchin Lane, and the umbrella shop which still housed the Excess Company – were hardly the length of a cricket pitch from Lloyd's in the Royal Exchange.

Another important event had come two years earlier. This was the setting up of the Pension Fund, under which staff members who had served a full forty years would get two-thirds of their salary at retirement as a pension. Nowadays such an arrangement may seem commonplace, but in the 1920s pension schemes were a novelty, and Heaths was among the earliest firms to start one.

With Cuthbert Heath spending more time in his office, the presiding genius at the box was now Montague Evans. He was not, recalls Percy Holford who came to the box in 1923, 'a technician in the sense underwriters have to be today. He wrote on flair.' At least part of the flair, despite his Welsh charm, lay in his some-what pessimistic outlook: besides his distaste for stockyard business, he hated writing cotton gins. Wooden buildings used for storing cotton crops, the gins were a high fire hazard: rates on them were often as high as 12 per cent on an insured value of $20,000. 'Evans, at Lloyd's, pulls a long face every time a loss comes in and points to "another cotton gin loss"', wrote Cuthbert Heath with evident amusement, 'but in these cases one is apt to overlook the premiums.' In fact the two men's underwriting methods could

This drawing by Hanslip Fletcher shows Cornhill from the Royal Exchange. Heaths had offices in Birchin Lane, the alley leading off Cornhill (*centre right*)

Mr. MONTAGUE. EVANS.

Montague Evans. A caricature kept by the Three Rooms Club at Lloyd's

hardly have been more different, and they rarely sat at the box together. 'Monty didn't trust himself not to be influenced by Heath's enthusiasm for having a go,' is George Thomson's revealing explanation.

The problems of writing commercial jewellery risks increased in the 1920s with a spate of a new type of crime made possible by motor-cars – the smash-and-grab raid. The first raid took place in 1924, at Harmans, the Bond Street jewellers. Part of the thieves' loot was an emerald necklace worth £8,000, and because of the publicity that followed, the crime was widely copied.

The period brought its quota of intriguing anecdotes of frauds, or attempted frauds, on jewellery underwriters. One of Heaths' clients was a Paris diamond merchant who was planning a selling trip to various business centres in south-western France. Arriving in Marseilles from Lyons, he was planning to go on to Toulouse and Bordeaux, returning from there to Paris. But when he got to Marseilles he found his pocket had been picked and that his wallet of diamonds was missing.

Percy Holford still remembers the loss adjuster's question to the dealer. 'Of course you didn't anticipate that you were going to be robbed?'
'Of course not.'
'Then why, if it was your intention to go on to Toulouse, did you take a Paris–Marseilles return ticket?

The startled dealer's reply was that he had bought the return ticket by mistake. The question had been a shot in the dark – but one that found its mark, says Mr Holford, for a return half from Marseilles would have been useless if he had completed his Bordeaux journey. It would have been useful only if he had known he was going to be robbed, or going to put up a pretence of being so.

The loss adjuster, whose suspicions were now firmly aroused, left instructions in his office that every time the dealer rang up, he was to be told that the adjuster was investigating a loss in Marseilles. 'Eventually the man's nerve broke,' recalls Mr Holford. 'He rang up to say he was pleased to report that he had found some of the diamonds, and the claim was therefore reduced. Eventually the adjuster went round and put it to him that it wouldn't be very nice for him if the underwriters doubted his word. With that he completely crumpled and withdrew it.'

Another case was that of a highly reputable Antwerp dealer, one of whose staff had gone on a diamond-selling trip to the Far East. The man went to Colombo and Singapore, not taking the diamonds on his person but sending them ahead by registered post, which was a common practice.

When he got to Singapore he found the package empty – it had been opened and then resealed. Heaths asked a loss adjuster to investigate, and the adjuster in turn employed a local agent. The local man analysed the wax of the replacement seals, then went to every stationer in Colombo and Singapore to see where the thief could have bought it. But it turned out that this particular type of sealing-wax was unobtainable in either city. 'Afterwards,' recalls Mr Holford, 'we found that it was a special sealing-wax which the

The 'Spirit of St Louis'

dealer used to buy in Antwerp to supply his staff. So we knew that the employee himself must have been the thief in this case.'

Meanwhile Cuthbert was, as always, exploring new areas of underwriting. In February, 1919 he had formed, with Sir Edward Mountain of the Eagle Star, a company called the British Aviation Insurance Association. Cuthbert Heath was chairman and his son Leopold, who had been demobilised on Christmas Eve, 1918, was secretary. The underwriter, who received a salary of £1,500 plus five per cent of profits, was an ex-RFC pilot named Captain Barber, an expert on technical aviation problems. Possibly Captain Barber was more expert on these than underwriting, for the experiment does not seem to have been a success. In April 1921, it was decided that the Association should accept no more risks 'in view of the fact that there seems to be no immediate future in aviation insurance and that there is no business to be had.' Lewis Angel chiefly remembers it because of an encounter with Cuthbert Heath:

> An ex-RFC pilot had called at the office and requested cover for a flight to England from France where he was going to buy one of the many surplus aircraft which the government was selling. But he would not know what type he would be buying until he had made his choice. He asked me to get him provisional cover and would send full details by post. I arranged this with Captain Barber, a postcard arrived with details, the premium was fixed and the insurance cover given. Presumably the aircraft had a safe passage, but the pilot never appeared at the

office again and requests for the premium sent to the address he had given were returned marked 'unknown'. Captain Barber was unwilling to waive the premium, so the firm was stuck with a bad debt of £40. I was sent for to give an explanation to Cuthbert Heath. He treated the matter as an immense joke, and dismissed me from his presence with a warning to 'beware of birdmen in the future'.

Cuthbert was to have more dealings with birdmen in the future, including the most famous of them all, Charles Lindbergh, whose 'Spirit of St Louis' was insured by Heaths for $18,000 on its return flight from Europe. As to the British Aviation Insurance Association, it would, as we shall see, before long return in a new guise. Meanwhile the 1920s were to see a revolutionary event which was to shape the whole future of reinsurance – the invention of the device known as the Burning Cost. This, like burglary insurance, was not his own invention. But like burglary insurance, it could not have happened without his constant willingness to embark on something new.

The importance of the Burning Cost system was that it replaced the previously immensely cumbersome procedure of writing treaty reinsurance. Till 1926 the traditional idea of a reinsurance was that every cession – the risk which the direct insurer 'cedes' to the reinsurer – should be listed separately and checked by the reinsurer. Because of the number of separate risks, these involved the use of huge sheets of paper known as bordereaux – complex and lengthy documents which often carried hundreds of entries. Nor was this all. Apart from the original entries, there were claims bordereaux, which had to be checked against the relative premium bordereaux, and others which included such alterations as dates of expiry, amendments of rates, and so on.

This process had long been seen as time-wasting and uneconomic. One of those who had sought a way round it was Guy Carpenter, the insurance manager of the Cotton Insurance Association of America, a pool of companies formed to insure and regulate the rates for fire and flood insurance on cotton warehouses. This pool had for many years carried excess of loss reinsurance, the premium being calculated on the claims experience in the past.

Carpenter's idea was that the same principle could be adapted to the fire portfolio of an insurance company. If the excess losses it had sustained over the previous five years could be related to its premium income, then surely, he thought, it would be possible to arrive at what he called the Burning Cost – the rate which the reinsurer ought to charge the company for the first year of a five-year contract? For the second year, the actual first year's experience would be added and the earliest year dropped, and so on until the contract became an entirely self-rated reinsurance – which would require no more detailed work than the noting of the re-assured company's annual premium income and past experience on the contract. Thus an easy annual adjustment would do away with the whole system of bordereaux and the detailed paperwork.

Having evolved his plan, Carpenter's next step was to try to sell it to the insurance markets, and in 1926 he came to London. Accounts vary as to when and where his first meeting with Cuthbert Heath took place. According to the best-known version, Cuthbert Heath and Carpenter met in London with Bissell, the president of the Hartford. Heath agreed to write the reinsurance on the lines suggested by Carpenter and then – suddenly getting doubts about whether he would be able to absorb the huge new flow of business – went off on holiday to Algeria where Carpenter followed him, eventually overcoming his misgivings.

This is the generally accepted story. But when Cuthbert died in 1939, the prominent New York insurance journal *Eastern Under-writer* printed, in the course of a long obituary, what it described as 'one of the most interesting stories told in London about Mr Heath'. According to this version, Carpenter came alone to London, and found nobody willing to write the business. The only person likely to do so, he was told, was Cuthbert Heath – but he was on a hunting holiday in Algeria. Carpenter then, according to the *Eastern Underwriter*, set off for Algeria and eventually ran Heath to earth at his camp in the interior of the country. Sitting in his tent, Heath listened carefully while Carpenter outlined his plan, and then replied:

> Mr Carpenter, you have done something which I have been trying to get American brokers to do for years. The average broker brings to me the cloth and says 'Mr Heath, would you not like to buy this cloth and make yourself a hat from it?' Now, you have made the hat; and you have brought it to me; you have put it on my head, and it fits.

Then, so the story continued, Heath took a piece of paper from his pocket, wrote on it that he would lead the risk and added his initial. 'Go back to London and show them this slip,' he told Carpenter. 'I am sure you will get a full list of underwriters.'

Over half a century later there is nobody alive in a position to know which is the likelier story. Perhaps the tent is an embellishment, but it is pleasant to think of one of the most highly technical insurance reforms of the century being hatched out by two men in a setting more reminiscent of a Foreign Legion romance than an underwriting office. And one point which seems not to ring true in the accepted version is that of Heath's agreeing to write the business

and then having second thoughts about it, for once Heath's mind was made up on something, he was absolute about it. Indecision of any kind was totally foreign to his nature.

The Surrey Union Hunt painted by F. A. Stewart. Cuthbert Heath is the tall figure in the centre

Whatever the facts about the meeting, the end of the episode is beyond doubt. Carpenter found that Cuthbert's promise was indeed the key to the London market. Within four years the Burning Cost system had completely replaced the old method of detailed bordereaux. One of the great advantages of the Carpenter Plan – or 'retro-formula' as it is sometimes known in modern markets – was that the new cover modified sharp variations of experience for the reinsurer, but there was another factor which was to bring even bigger premiums to London. Because Cuthbert Heath had cautiously specified a limit of $200,000 on any one loss, irrespective of the number of risks involved, the direct insurers found themselves needing to take out further excess policies to cover themselves against the possibility of a major catastrophe which would expose them to a spread of many risks. Soon the companies were taking out excess covers over and above the Burning Cost reinsurance, of many millions of dollars against fire catastrophes as well as riot, civil commotion and windstorm damage. Cuthbert Heath's 'Why not?' had once more pushed back the frontiers of insurance and in doing so earned vast sums of premium for the London market.

The post-war decade brought Cuthbert both public and private honours. One that gave him special pleasure was his appointment as joint master of the Surrey Union Hunt, the other being his

Mr. CUTHBERT E. HEATH, O.B.E.

friend and neighbour Harry Lee Steere, of Ockley. Though not as prestigious as some of the famous Midlands hunts, its houndwork was said to have been admired by the Duke of Beaufort. And during Cuthbert's mastership, at least, it was noted for its stirrup-cups: he used to regale the huntsmen with draughts of one of his own favourites, Imperial Tokay, though his niece Mrs Edwin Wood's impression at the time was that most of them did not appreciate what they were getting.

He received countless appeals from charities, and few went unheeded. Lloyd's charities and its traditions had a special place in his affections, and in 1918 he had made a major contribution to the Nelson Room, Lloyd's collection of the silver originally given in gratitude to Nelson and his captains, when he bought back the silver vase presented to Captain Edward Rotheram, who commanded the *Royal Sovereign* at Trafalgar.

In 1920 he was made an OBE and in 1925 became High Sheriff of

ABOVE 'Mr. Cuthbert E. Heath, O.B.E.' from a series of caricatures at the Lloyd's Three Rooms Club

OPPOSITE Heath drinks a stirrup cup with Harry Lee Steere, joint master of the Surrey Union Hunt

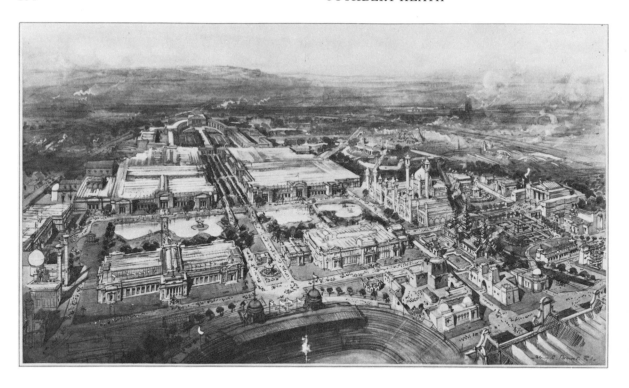

The British Empire
Exhibition, 1924.
Buildings included
Palaces of Industry,
Art, Engineering,
Religious Art and
others dedicated to
countries of the British
Empire

Surrey. At Lloyd's, in 1921, he was presented with the portrait by
Sir William Orpen commissioned by members of his syndicate,
and perhaps for the first time became aware that he was held in
something more than admiration. With all his qualities, said
Sidney Boulton at the presentation dinner,

> we love best in him the patience, the fairness, the kindliness, and the
> gentleness that never fail amid all the hurry and worry of our daily work
> ... Cuthbert Heath, you are an old darling and we all love you.

The market's affection was to be visibly demonstrated in 1924,
the year of the British Empire Exhibition. Despite the fact that
exhibitions usually turned out to be expensive risks for the insurer,
Heath was firmly of the view that Lloyd's should, as a goodwill
gesture, guarantee the Exhibition without asking any premium.
For its aim was, he wrote,

> to serve more than one object. It relieves unemployment and it will be
> the means of bringing many visitors and much money to this country –
> besides promoting trade. It is felt that not only should Lloyd's be willing
> to help where others have done so, but that in view of the great interest
> felt in the Exhibition by the Prince of Wales it would be a nice thing to
> give this guarantee to him as some acknowledgement from Lloyd's of all
> he has done.

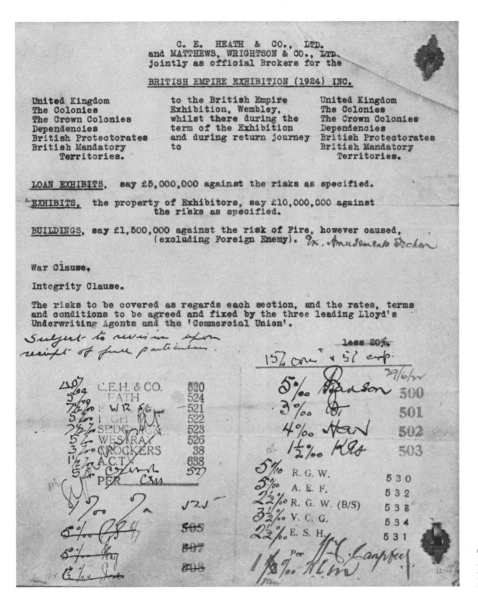

The Lloyd's slip for the British Empire Exhibition

Heath not only promoted the idea in the market but, on one memorable day, broked the risk himself in the Room. He was now sixty-five and for several years had not been seen in the Room since increasing deafness had led to his transacting business in his office. His second cousin, Philip Heath, recalled the unusual event:

One afternoon business was proceeding at Lloyd's in its usual decorous way. An underwriter happened to look up and noticed a tall, stooping figure standing patiently in a queue waiting his turn to see a leading underwriter: and this was only right and proper, for at Lloyd's it is a rigid rule that everyone, whether a leading broker or a junior clerk,

must take his turn in the queue with the others. With a shout the underwriter left his box and ran across the Room to greet Mr Heath the broker
(not Mr Heath the famous underwriter) waiting to show the Empire
Exhibition risk to a leading underwriter.

Others had seen him too, and pandemonium broke out. All business
at Lloyd's stopped. Underwriters threw aside their books and rushed to
join the crowd round the rather bewildered old gentleman. They were
cheering him, they were patting him on the back, they were trying to
shake his hand, they were telling him how wonderful it was to have him
among them again after all this time. The demonstration lasted for
several minutes – then Lloyd's went back to work and Cuthbert went on
with his job. The queue in which he had been standing mysteriously disappeared so that he was in front of the underwriter. The latter glanced
at the slip on which details of the proposed guarantee were shown, wrote
down a large line on behalf of the syndicate he represented and initialled
it. Then, with a broad smile he said 'Nothing for you to pay, Mr Heath.'
He crossed out the proposed rate shown on the slip and substituted '0%'.

Cuthbert thanked him politely and went on to see the other underwriters. Each time the queue disappeared and every underwriter wrote
his line, large or small, according to the size of his syndicate. All these
hardheaded business men knew perfectly well that they were bound to
face a heavy loss on the policy and they couldn't care less. This was their
way of showing their affection . . . The underwriters at Lloyd's had every
reason to be proud of the way in which they behaved on that famous day.
It was perhaps their finest hour.

Steadily and sedately he was blossoming into a grand old man. In
1928 he became Deputy Lieutenant of Surrey and though he still
came to the office – somewhat to the anxiety of Montague Evans,
who regarded his increasingly tolerant attitude as an underwriting
hazard – he began to spend more time on wider interests. Credit
insurance continued to be his favourite, and since the mid-1920s
the Trade Indemnity Company had been instrumental in arranging
European conferences on the subject. In April 1928 he wrote to his
daughter Genesta, now married and living in Kenya:

Last week was a very busy one. There was the International Credit
Insurance meeting in Paris, attended by 15 nationalities and the open
meeting by quite 200 people, including 30 French bankers. There were
speeches innumerable and lunches and dinners galore. It was a great
success and I think we have done a great deal of good work. I was the
President but resigned the chairmanship of the meeting to our French
colleagues – and was very glad to as I could not keep pace with all the
French talk.

In the same letter he described the new offices of the Excess
Company. These were in Lime Street, just across the road from the

new Lloyd's building. Another Lloyd's event referred to in the same letter was the publication of Wright and Fayle's history of Lloyd's which, he noted,

> has taken about 3 years to write. There are several pages about your humble servant and he is called 'one of the two most remarkable men who have made Lloyd's what it is in the last 40 years'!!! There's swank for you, but I know you like to hear these things.

This apparently unruffled surface was not without its ripples. Indeed something approaching a storm blew up in 1928 over Cuthbert's proposal to take over another broker's – the Leeds firm of A. W. Bain and Son, whose chairman, Sir Ernest Bain, had an ambition to shine in the more glittering Lloyd's market. Bains themselves were not Lloyd's brokers, but they had a considerable array of business on their books, including woollen mills in Yorkshire, industrial fire risks in the Midlands, and above all the prestigious firm of Unilever as a client.

It was a prospect that seems to have made a strong impression on Cuthbert. Owning fifty-one per cent of the shares in Heaths, he entered into a deal with the Bains without consulting his fellow-directors: under it, Sir Ernest Bain and his brother John were to be members of the Heath board. When Cuthbert broke the news it was greeted with dismay by the entire board, with the exception of Arthur Burns, who preferred the idea of expanding domestic and Continental business to the American side, which he distrusted.

Basically the opposition to the takeover came from two of Heaths' top brokers, William Pryce and George Bagley. Both were directors in charge of the rapidly expanding American side, and they saw the Bain link not only as blocking their own prospects but as a diversion away from the key area of American business.

Meanwhile there was another side to the situation which Cuthbert and Burns seem not to have considered. This was the emergence of C. T. Bowring as a massive rival for Heaths' US business. The insurance department of Bowrings, which had begun in the eighteenth century as a Newfoundland trading and shipping firm, had only recently come to the fore as a leading broking house. Now, under a brilliant insurance chief, Sir William Hargreaves, Bowrings were threatening Heaths' American business. Four years earlier they had recruited one of Heaths most experienced underwriters, Matthew Drysdale. Now Hargreaves wanted to win over Bagley because of his extensive American connections.

None of this seems to have been known to Heath and Arthur Burns when on 3 January 1928, Burns received a joint letter of

resignation from Bagley, Pryce, and the company secretary, A. J. McMin. The three spoke of 'grave misgivings as to our own security and prospects of advancement looking to the future'. The presence of 'two gentlemen from outside the organisation' – in other words, the Bains – created, the letter said, an entirely new state of affairs in the firm 'whereby our natural aspirations to enlarge our holdings and responsibilities in the business which we have helped to build up have received a distinct setback.'

The first week of January 1928 brought snow and heavy rain – a suitable background for the flu season, and Burns was confined to his Essex home on doctor's orders. Cuthbert Heath, at Anstie, seems to have received the resignations later, for it was not until 6 January that Burns received a letter conveying his reaction. Evidently Cuthbert was in favour of some kind of compromise, for Burns wrote from his sickbed that if Cuthbert 'seriously proposed reinstating these fellows', he could no longer undertake the responsibility of conducting the office.

Cuthbert's letter must also have contained a proposal to promote Merrick Tylor of the Excess to the position of a life director. Burns' reply to this was wary. Tylor would be 'a great strength' to the firm, he continued,

> *But* I cannot agree to this appointment merely as a condition precedent to some bargain with the three malcontents. I am not writing thus firmly under the influence of physical circumstances or of any other pressure.

Soon correspondence was pouring from Burns' sickbed headquarters like orders of the day put out by some beleaguered general. On the 8th he wrote five separate letters to Montague Evans alone. By now he certainly knew of the impending defection for 'assuming that they go tomorrow,' he told Evans,

> I think we ought to cable to every American client as follows: 'Directors Pryce and Bagley no longer in any way connected with this firm.' There would probably be a code word for the last two lines.

The longest of the five letters contained, less dramatically, his own proposals for the reorganisation that must follow. L. J. Taylor, he thought, would become American director, 'with Gould and Squire as his lieutenants.'

After that the hectic correspondence ceases. The resignation of the three was 'noted with regret' at a Board meeting three days later. Robert North, who had been with Heaths since the Winchester House days, was made company secretary succeeding McMin. In the event Bagley took half the business of one major

client, a Philadelphia reinsurance broker, to Bowrings, and for the next decade the two firms were to remain the predominant contenders for American non-marine business at Lloyd's. It was the beginning of a new age in which Lloyd's brokers, competing with each other in technical expertise as well as knowledge of their own market, were to bring an ever-increasing service to their clients.

But it was a young man's world. And that summer Cuthbert Heath was approaching seventy. His visits to London, except for board meetings, became less frequent, though July found him sitting in the Law Courts – 'about the most comfortable place in London in this weather as it is quite cool and nice except for hard seats' – over a case relating to forest fire insurance. Meanwhile there was no dimming of his old, spry, commanding manner, if we can judge by his brisk reply to John Bain, who had evidently suggested that the Excess Company should be sold. 'My dear John Bain,' Cuthbert wrote on 3 July,

> If it is a question of the foreign Cos. buying the Excess I am afraid the idea must be ruled out. It would destroy the associations which the Excess has formed in many directions, it would imply complete changes in the Staff and its outlook and finally we believe the Excess has still a considerable future to look forward to.
>
> Also the fact that we have the Excess as a background is of considerable value to the Brokerage firm and also to the underwriters.
>
> So for all these reasons, I don't think we ought to consider a change. On the other hand I have been thinking that if you and your brother have cash to spare it might be a good thing if you held some shares in the Excess. It would give you an interest in its prosperity and I really believe it is a good investment.

The reply was inspired, perhaps, by a more than usually affectionate feeling towards the company he had founded thirty-four years earlier, for the Excess had recently commissioned a portrait of him by the artist John Hay. A slight difficulty seems to have arisen halfway through the sittings, when the company decided that they wanted Cuthbert shown in his deputy lieutenant's khaki. 'Poor man, he had to alter the black city coat he had put on me,' was Cuthbert's considerate comment.

More than ever in his old age, he continued to captivate everyone who met him. Among those who sensed his personal charm was Lord Cobbold, who recalls being 'produced for him to inspect' in 1929 before going to work for the Excess Company in Italy: 'One of the directors said 'He's a bit young, isn't he?' Cuthbert Heath chuckled and said "That's one thing he'll grow out of."'

When he got to Italy, Cameron Cobbold, as he then was, found the name of Heath – usually pronounced as 'Cootbert Eat' – worked

Sikorsky S64
Skycrane operated by
Evergreen Helicopters
Inc. Helicopter
insurance is one of the
specialist skills of
C. E. Heath & Co

as a talisman. 'It didn't cut much ice if you said you were a London insurance man. What made them listen was when you said you were Cootbert Eat's man.' Cameron Cobbold's stay with the Excess lasted for four years: in 1933, Cuthbert's old friend and admirer, Montague Norman, asked him if he would mind releasing Cobbold to take up an important post in the Bank of England's foreign department. Cuthbert took the request as a compliment to his skilful picking of bright young men: the insurance industry lost a potential talent and the Bank acquired a future Governor.

In November 1929 Cuthbert went to Paris as British representative on the League of Nations insurance committee, where he was irritated by the long-windedness of the officials which would mean, he feared, a further session later. But to make up for it there were long days at Anstie, and the society of Genesta's children, over on holiday from Kenya: always anxious to encourage specialist skills, he noted with pleasure that they had become 'ardent butterfly hunters'. To add to the interest of the pursuit, he not only bought them cork-line boxes, setting boards and nets, but searched everywhere for a book on the butterflies of Kenya, eventually running one to earth at the Zoo Library. That November there were three days' shooting, and the opening meet of the season for the Surrey Union. Cuthbert had a new cream-coloured horse named Custard, and gave a breakfast attended by sixty local farmers, being much amused by 'one old fellow who arrived an hour before everyone else and sat steadily eating, with the whisky bottle at his elbow, until everyone else had finished.'

He had always been deeply devoted to the Leith Hill area, and in 1929 he became alerted to the perils of its being built on when another local landowner proposed to sell sixty acres near Friday Street Ponds. 'A regular "do" I call it,' wrote Cuthbert to Genesta in Africa. 'He frightens the public into subscribing to prevent it and gets about three times the proper value. I wouldn't subscribe a penny.'

The refusal to have anything to do with his neighbour's tactics was characteristic. So was the gesture that promptly followed – Cuthbert decided to give two hundred acres of his own estate, the lands near the summit of Leith Hill known as Duke's Warren, to the National Trust.

> We should all hate to see it built upon, and with the price paid £120 an acre for the Friday Street site it might well be that they might charge my estate with death duties on the Warren at a value of £20,000 whereas I only paid £80 for it! So I am making a virtue out of a necessity and handing it over. After all I shall still get just what I am getting from the place now and it will give enormous pleasure to a lot of people for ever I hope.

Heath's Condor, the 77ft sloop sponsored by C. E. Heath & Co in the Whitbread Round-the-World Race in 1977

ABOVE *Anne of Anstie.*
Heath made his first
venture into the family
sailing tradition with
this yacht

BELOW This photo-
graph of Cuthbert is
surrounded by his
drawings of Anstie at
various dates in
its history

Anne's Anstie

Anstie 1886.

Anstie
1930

For some time now he and Sarah had taken to wintering in the south. 'We are off to St Raphael for our usual two months or so,' he wrote in January 1929 to Sir Raymond Beck, his old friend from the wartime aircraft damage committee. Another favourite spot was the Hotel Méditerranée at Cannes, where he was flattered to be invited to join the millionaires' golf club. But the Mediterranean visits had stirred something deeper in him, a chord which had remained silent almost since his boyhood: in November 1929 he mentions, for the first time, the possibility of buying a yacht named the *Anna Marie*. The owner wanted to keep the name for a new boat he was planning. Cuthbert, with characteristic energy for researching the facts, had been musing on a new one:

> We think 'Ann of Anstie' would be a good name. It comes from the records of Surrey. About 1450 it is recorded that certain people were fined for letting their cattle stray. The only two people I could identify were 'John of Pinkhurst' (an old farm of Harry Steere's near Oakwood Hill) and 'Ann of Anstie'. They both had to pay about 1s.

By December the deal with the owner of the *Anna Marie* was evidently closed, for we find Cuthbert writing to a Cowes boat-builder named Drover on the subject of bilge keels and having the yacht coppered. Clearly he had not lost any of his zest for innovation, for in the letter to Drover he mentioned that he had 'seen two things lately'.

> One is the spraying of metal on wood by a new process which is being used by shipbuilders, and another is the employment of rustless steel for under water surfaces. I am wondering whether instead of coppering I might have rustless steel sprayed on the yacht's hull. Do you know anything about it or shall I consult Lloyd's Register?

But there was one aspect on which he was certainly in no need of Mr Drover's advice. 'I think I will take out my own insurance', he courteously but firmly added.

At seventy he was recapturing the excitement of a schoolboy. The great non-marine underwriter was at long last returning to the sea, his first love.

CHAPTER SIX

'Il voit jusqu'au bout'

In the summer of 1930 Cuthbert's great preoccupation was with the *Anne of Anstie*, and in July he set off on a modest cruise round the Isle of Wight and up the Beaulieu river, wearing 'my beautiful RYS uniform'. The latter gave him particular satisfaction: the Royal Yacht Squadron in those days had the reputation of being inclined to pick and choose its members, and Cuthbert had had some anxiety that he might be rejected on the grounds of being 'in trade'. Sarah did not accompany him: now suffering severely from rheumatism, she had been undergoing intensive treatment in Guy's Hospital which, he wrote to Genesta on 27 July, 'is supposed to have destroyed all the noxious tissues between the joints and now fresh and healthy tissues are to take their place. Anyway we are full of hope.'

The summer must have been a hectic one, for the week after the Isle of Wight cruise the Heaths moved out of Aldford Street. Sarah's convalescence had not been helped by the noise of building operations at Grosvenor House, then in process of construction. But the Heaths had evidently not yet decided on another permanent London house, for in the first week of August they moved to a rented flat in Whitehall Court.

Probably Sarah's illness was one reason for the temporary nature of the move. Another was that the Heaths were now planning a more ambitious project. This was the purchase of La Domaine de Savaric, a small estate comprising a farmhouse and several acres of precipitous terrain at Eze, in the Alpes-Maritimes. The house had half a dozen bedrooms and a magnificent view over the Mediterranean. Five minutes from the sea as the crow flies, it was more than half an hour by car. Mrs Joan Sarll recalls that:

> Savaric was modelled on a Provencal farmhouse and was utterly charming. It was on a steep hill, and one entered the back on the upper storey, going down to the dining and sitting rooms. Sarah was able to give rein to her love of all things French. She discovered an *atelier* near Versailles where they made good copies of Versailles furniture, and the house was mostly furnished thus. It had a beautiful mountain garden and CEH planted many trees. I visited Savaric seven years ago. All the cypress trees had grown up round the back of the house and it was even more delightful.

PREVIOUS PAGE A view of Eze and *La Côte d'Azur*

Sarah seems usually to have been the prime mover in planning a visit to Eze. Cuthbert was a more moderate Francophile: possibly the fact had an unconscious influence on his somewhat Churchillian French accent. Once, when lost in the mountains, he stopped his car to ask a passing labourer the way to Marseilles. He repeated the request several times in his best French, only to receive the reply from the bewildered local 'Monsieur, je regrette que je ne comprends pas l'anglais.'

The plans for the purchase of Savaric must have been complete by October 1930, for in that month he sent a photograph of the house to Genesta in Kenya. Meanwhile life was not only a matter of moving house. 'If you read *The Times*,' he wrote in the same letter, 'you will see a letter from me in big print on the subject of helping trade. I suggested to *The Times* that they should take up the idea themselves, but the Editor asked me to write an official letter.' The letter – it was indeed in the big print which the paper in those days reserved for its more important correspondence – suggested, perhaps a little optimistically, that the country would be better off if labour could be persuaded to submit to a ten per cent cut in

Cuthbert Heath as an old man at Eze

wages with a view to helping exports. The following month saw a potentially more fruitful venture – a meeting with President Masaryk of Czechoslovakia, who wanted Cuthbert's help in setting up a credit insurance company in his country.

Meanwhile life continued pleasantly at Eze. Sarah used to go to the casino in the morning, and in the afternoons there would be a family drive, often with their grandchildren. Cuthbert, Mrs Joan Sarll remembers,

> used to play golf with Phillips Oppenheim at Montagel. He called CEH the Father of Lloyd's and CEH called him the Father of Lies. The drives were often to see some old church or beauty spot, or along the coast. I remember being thrilled once at driving to the Italian border and actually seeing Italy.

Sometimes there would be visits from world insurance leaders who made long journeys to Eze to see him. His daughter Genesta recalls one Frenchman who came to Savaric from New York. On his arrival, he remained deep in conversation with her father for half an hour, then emerged saying that it was time for him to begin his journey back to America. When Genesta expressed astonishment that he had come such a long way for so brief a meeting, the man told her that, for his business, half an hour with her father was more than worth it. 'Il voit jusqu'au bout,' he told her. The phrase could serve to sum up his whole career, for Cuthbert always saw through to the end of any problem. Even in old age, his mind was a powerful flashlight illuminating the darkest tunnel.

Cuthbert Heath aboard his yacht

By now he had found a skipper for the *Anne*. This was a colourful retired admiral named Candy, later to be nicknamed 'Monte Carlo's darling' by Sarah Heath because of his exuberant habit of giving lobster and champagne parties on board the *Anne* while she and Cuthbert were away in England. Admiral Candy must have brought his new command through the Bay of Biscay by the early spring of 1931, for that April he and Cuthbert were playing golf at Cagnes, and the following month fishing off Corsica in the yacht. Nowhere is Cuthbert's tenderness for the living world more sharply revealed than in one letter written from the island:

> We had a lovely smooth trip coming here but it was foggy and the bird migration must have been going on as three swallows came and perched on board, a hawk, and a dear little willow-wren which took up its quarters for the night under a cushion in the saloon. Poor thing it was dead in the morning. Admiral C. in the kindness of his heart put out bread for the swallows! It is curious how people can go through life without knowing anything about nature.

'I think people get a mania for writing letters as they get older,' he wrote a few months later. Thanks to the fact, we have a more complete picture of Cuthbert's later years than of almost any other period. Often the letters are chatty and descriptive: one day it is impossible to get into Monte Carlo because the streets are shut off for 'the automobile racing' and another day the news is that the Aga Khan has beaten the Commander-in-Chief of the Mediterranean Fleet at golf. Sometimes the letters are more personal: evidently Genesta had protested about his custom of signing his letters 'y.a.f. C.H.' which stood for 'your affectionate father Cuthbert Heath'. Her protest drew this from Cuthbert:

> How would you like me to sign? 'Your devoted Cuthbert'? The other way is shorter, dignified and sufficiently indicative of affection and altogether I think I will stick to it ... We are having brilliant weather now. It is almost too hot to walk about, in the middle of the day at all events. Y.A. Father. How will that do?

1932 saw the move to what was to be the Heaths' last permanent home in London. This was a small flat – by their standards – in the Manor, a charming house on the west side of Davies Street in Mayfair. After a holiday in Scotland the Heaths moved there in September. 'The paint smell has gone, so we have a roof in London over our heads again and the whole flat is much improved.'

But neither London nor Eze ever evoked quite such enthusiasm as he felt for Anstie. Off and on till 1937 he was to remain joint master of the Surrey Union, and in 1932 he had a new horse called Goliath – probably with reason, for Cuthbert's stature meant that he always needed a heavyweight hunter. Later there was also a new dog – 'very good looking and affectionate but I'm afraid he is not much of a retriever. He has taken four prizes for looks but he seems very young for his age and does not know how to pick up a pheasant.'

Perhaps it was a sign of his continuing zest for life that his deafness did not get worse with age. Indeed, thanks to a new hearing device, he sometimes felt it was better than it had ever been. Listening to church music on the radio from Florence with its help was, he wrote from Eze in 1934, 'quite a revelation'. Because of the improvement, he and Sarah planned to go to Sunday morning service at the Eglise du Port in Nice 'where they say the music is very good,' and on the way back from church he planned 'a run on the roughest road we can find to test the new shock absorbers we have had fitted to the Rolls Royce.' Whether it was shock-absorbers, deaf aids or insurance, his zeal for constantly trying out new things never left him.

Cuthbert with a young riding enthusiast. He is seen wearing his hearing-aid in this picture

There was also evidently some thought of a new yacht to replace the *Anne*, for in the same letter he speaks of Candy going to Toulon 'to flatten his nose' against another and larger yacht which had been lying in port there. 'But it is ten to one against anything happening. With seven grandchildren crying for bread I feel I must be careful.' The comment may seem a trifle eccentric, coming from someone whose annual income was over £60,000. Probably it expressed the anxieties of an ageing man, for it was far from characteristic: Cuthbert had none of the closeness over money to be found in so many rich men. If anything his attitude to it was vague to a point where it must often have been irritating to others – as when he once told one of his younger underwriters that he 'ought to have a house in Belgrave Square'. Cuthbert's generosity was equal to his vagueness: on being told that the underwriter couldn't

A family group in 1932

afford to live in Belgrave Square on his salary, he promptly saw to it that the salary was doubled.

In old age his attitude to money was most often just as casual. On his increasingly rare visits to the office, Arthur Fowler, his private secretary, used to put a poundsworth of silver in his pocket when he went out. 'They give me this, I don't know what for,' was Cuthbert's comment. But perhaps the most acute and personal thing he ever said about money was when he told his daughter that he found it rather sad that, however much he gave away, it never seemed to make any difference to him.

In November 1935 he wrote to his daughter Genesta with unconcealed pleasure:

It is rather a secret until the 20th when there is a general meeting of Lloyd's but last week the Chairman asked to see me and said it was 'the unanimous and enthusiastic' wish of the committee that I should allow them to have my portrait painted to be hung in the Library at Lloyd's in recognition of my services to it. There are only three others (one being of Angerstein, a great man of about 1820), so it is a very fine compliment. They asked me to choose an artist so I said John Hay – at least he knows his subject.

It was an historic moment. Cuthbert was now in the pantheon of Lloyd's, his pioneering work done and non-marine insurance prospering throughout the market. In another sense, as he of all people knew, the revolution he had begun was only at its beginning. New kinds of insurances would become necessary as man took new steps to improve his relationship to the world about him. Construction, transport, aviation were some of the new areas but there would be many others.

It was thanks to the genius of Cuthbert Heath that as these new risks and demands for cover came along, the market would almost automatically find the flexibility to insure them.

Insurance proceeds a little like a ship taking echo-soundings. Sometimes a new invention or technique seems likely to produce a new area of business. If so, insurers will set up a listening-post or even a stall in the market to try to see whether the new idea will, in insurance terms, produce a book of business. Sometimes such a move will be seen to be premature, and the insurance interest will fade, often reappearing later.

Something of this kind had happened, as we saw, with the new area of aviation. The British Aviation Insurance Association had ceased underwriting in 1921 on the ground that aircraft insurance had no immediate future. Now, as commercial aviation began to be part of everyday life instead of a nine days' wonder, both Lloyd's and the companies were taking an increasing interest, and the

A dinner held at the Savoy in 1934 for the staff of C. E. Heath & Co Limited

early 1930s saw the revival of the Association under the name of the British Aviation Insurance Group, whose capital was a hundred shares of one pound each, divided between C. E. Heath and Co. and the Union Insurance Society of Canton. This somewhat token gesture towards aviation insurance became much more positive in 1931, when the Group was again reorganized, this time under the name of the British Aviation Insurance Company, and the capital increased to £250,000. The new shareholders included seven major insurance companies of which the Royal, Commercial Union and the North British and Mercantile held 40,000 each while Montague Evans, representing Heaths, held 39,950.

As with the British Aviation Insurance Association, the underwriter of the new company was a former aviator, this time a Captain Lamplugh. At first the underwriting results were good, and over the period 1931–3 the company made £80,000. 1934 and 1935 were leaner years, due to a mixture of inadequate rates and the economic situation, but by 1936 the problem seems to have been mastered, for the chairman, Sir Arthur Worley, was able to report that 'our persistent efforts to raise rates were meeting with some measure of reward'.

As so often with the insurance business, cheap rates and tough competition seem to have been more of a cause of bad results than claims. In the England-Melbourne Air Race of 1934 the company earned a net premium of £500 with no losses sustained. Three years later, when the Hindenburg airship was destroyed by fire at Lakehurst, the company's line was one-fortieth of a total insurance cover of £488,000, but thanks to skilful reinsurance, the net loss to the company was only just over £1,000 on the hull and £1,500 for liability insurance.

The British Aviation Insurance Company was closely involved with aviation underwriters in other countries, and in June 1934 there came a major step forward. A meeting was held at the Company's Threadneedle Street office, attended by aviation underwriters from nine other European countries. Its objects, according to the minutes, were

> to constitute an official body which shall be able to speak and negotiate on behalf of aviation insurance interests, to provide a central office for the circulation of information between members, to co-operate for the better regulation and conduct of aviation insurance, and generally to do all such things as may be beneficial to the development and conduct of this branch of insurance.

The result of the Threadneedle Street meeting was the formation of the International Union of Aviation Insurers, which still remains

ABOVE The famous *Hindenberg*. Last of the great airships of the 1930s, it was destroyed by fire at Lakehurst in 1937

OPPOSITE Early aeroplanes. The British Aviation Insurance Group was revived in the 1930s when aviation became part of everyday life

the leading international body in its market. The historic link with the union is one of which Heaths remains particularly proud. Recently it was reinforced when David Barham, Heaths' chief underwriter, became president of the Union which now has members in thirty-three different countries.

A somewhat less happy venture in the 1930s was motor underwriting. As brokers, Heaths had been building up an increasingly valuable motor account since the early 'twenties. Much of the business had been placed with the Excess Company, though as the availability of cheap motoring spread, there were soon a number of motor syndicates at Lloyd's. In 1930 the new Road Traffic Act made third party cover obligatory, and the market found itself inundated with new business.

Probably it was with the new Act in mind that Montague Evans decided to widen the Heath underwriting empire by buying up a small syndicate which was already trading at Lloyd's as A1 Motor Policies. (From the earliest days of motor insurance, the motor syndicates had been allowed, unlike others, to have names which would make them recognizable to the general public.) Lewis Angel, who had till now been concerned with motor broking, was appointed underwriter – somewhat to his consternation, for as

a broker he had regarded the syndicate as among the less successful. The office he inherited, he recalls,

> was two small rooms on one of the lower floors of Lloyd's building, and there was also a seat in one of the underwriting boxes. I had a look at the filing system which was not at all bad, considering the general amateur set-up. I was appalled by the stationery, all of which was printed on the most bilious looking paper ... I resolved at once to change this to something more in keeping with the dignity of Heath and Co.

The bilious stationery was the least of Angel's problems, for Montague Evans seems to have neglected the fact that a motor syndicate needs to issue policies, claim forms and certificates – to be, in effect, a miniature insurance company. As regards the actual underwriting, says Mr Angel:

> It was soon clear to me that I was going to spend as much time getting rid of business already on the books as in attracting new policy holders. One or two brokers were having things very much their own way, and were using muscle to obtain acceptance of risks which, as a broker, I. would have been ashamed to show to underwriters. Moreover these and many other brokers had been given authority to grant temporary cover and issue temporary Road Traffic Act certificates. Large quantities of books of certificates had been supplied to them, which through the intermediary of their sub-agents, had fetched up in the hands of all sorts of motor dealers up and down the country. No records had been kept of them and it was quite impossible to recall them. Even after the syndicate closed down, certificates were still being issued by garages in the remote bogs of Ireland.

A further problem was that one of the brokers concerned had arranged a special policy for members of the RAC at specially reduced rates: there were many such schemes in the motor market, and generally the broker was content to accept a lower commission as a contribution to the special terms. This, Angel discovered, was not so in the case of the RAC policy:

> But there was little I could do about it since the broker in question was a name on the syndicate. I consoled myself with the thought that perhaps members of the RAC were a cut above the ordinary motorist, although I could not see why they should be better drivers. But I had grave doubts about the wisdom of the scheme, since even if it did show a profit on its own, it still had to contribute to the general profit.
>
> The problem blew up in my face one Sunday morning when I opened my paper and was confronted by a large advertisement offering associate membership of the RAC with reduced privileges, but with the advantage of the cheaper insurance cover. The subscription was £2 which was well within the saving obtained from the special insurance

scheme. I spent most of that day walking on Hampstead Heath wondering what on earth I was going to do about it and what was to be the effect of this new class of assured on the scheme in general.

I protested, but without effect. I regret very much to say that I received no backing from Mr Evans, who seemed to have a complete blind spot in regard to the syndicate and its affairs.

For five years Angel and his team struggled on in a vain attempt to make the underwriting viable and provide the kind of service to the customers which would be appropriate to a syndicate owned by Cuthbert Heath. But the problems were too great, and at the end of 1938 the syndicate ceased underwriting. What persuaded Evans to acquire it in the first place, or, having done so, not to allow it proper resources, remains a mystery. Whatever the reason, the episode was one of Heaths' few underwriting failures.

The major broking houses tend to encircle Lloyd's like tugs swirling round a liner. Following the market's move to East India House, Heaths in turn acquired the lease of part of the new Bankside House in Leadenhall Street. The Excess, meanwhile, remained in Birchin Lane, where it was presided over by Merrick Tylor, who had now run it for twenty years since Cuthbert Heath had first installed him in the umbrella shop.

Tylor was by all accounts an autocratic, not to say daunting figure. According to Mr S. H. Van Geuns, then a partner in the firm of Langeveldt-Schroder which represented the Excess in Holland and the Dutch East Indies, 'an hour with Tylor was a most exhausting thing. He was an extremely clever man. He could ask more difficult questions in a minute than any other human being,' while Lewis Angel remembers that:

> he and I crossed swords because I complained to him that I used to take him proposals for Employers' Liability but was never allowed to discuss them – I always had to leave them with him. I said to him, 'You don't want a broker to do this, you want an errand boy.' He just said, 'I'm sorry, that's the way I'm going to do it.'

Tylor's formal and majestic methods extended far beyond his underwriting. One story tells how he was visited by Cornelius Reid, a well-known New York broker. The visitor was invited for the weekend to Tylor's country house. Towards the end of the second day Tylor told him: 'Mr Reid, we have now got to know each other quite well. The time has come for us to call each other Reid and Tylor.'

If he took a visiting broker to the theatre, Tylor would book three seats – the third being for his overcoat. One foreign broker

went with him to the races: Tylor told him they would be going on a
particular train, and the visiting broker took the precaution of
checking that the train would stop at the station which served the
racecourse. According to the timetable it did not. He pointed this
out to Tylor who simply said, 'It will.' It turned out that he had
arranged for the train to make a special stop there. But the most
remarkable Tylor story comes from Mr Van Geuns:

> Before the war I had a friend in Cologne who was a German Jewish
> doctor. At first he did not believe what the Nazis would do, and he had
> not tried to get permission to go as a refugee to England. Then one day
> they came and smashed all his equipment and killed his neighbour, and
> he asked me to help him to get to England. I thought of Tylor, and wrote
> him a letter, asking if he could possibly get permission for my friend. For
> three weeks there was no answer and I thought he must be furious. Then
> I got a letter. He'd been to the Foreign Office to see the Secretary of State
> and got permission for my friend to come to England. Partly it was
> generosity, but Tylor was also a very vain man. I think he wanted to
> show that he could do something which no one else could do.

With all his eccentricities, Tylor was an extremely able underwriter. The company he ran on Cuthbert Heath's behalf was in
itself an unusual structure, which bore much more resemblance
to a Lloyd's syndicate than to a conventional insurance company.
Its underwriting was closely interwoven with that of the Heath
syndicate, which wrote much of its reinsurance. Often a risk would
be led by Tylor and the balance written by Evans at the box.

In the 1930s the organization as a whole was increasingly expanding into foreign business, and here the links were even closer.
Heaths' contract department, whose job was to handle overseas
treaties, worked in parallel with the Excess, which had by now
appointed overseas agents in several countries.

Insurance is often said to be the most international of all forms
of business, and there are two reasons why this should be so. One
is reinsurance, which means that an insurer in one country may
offload part of his exposure in the markets of several other countries.
The second is the agency system, under which an underwriter in
one country will let another 'use his pen', as the market phrase
goes, to write business in his name up to an agreed limit. The
earliest Excess agency agreement had been signed in 1903 by
Cuthbert Heath. It gave authority to Alfred Schroder in Amsterdam
to write insurance on behalf of Heaths, and confirmed '5 per cent
brokerage to yourself and 20 per cent of the yearly net profits.'
By the 1930s the scope of this type of international operation had
spread to include India, New Zealand, Belgium, Denmark and

Norway: thanks to Eric Irgens, who was now head of the international contracts department, Heaths was said to have the largest book in London of Scandinavian reinsurance. But links with some of the more far-flung agencies were still remote. When Mr John Cope of the contracts department was sent by Tylor to Shanghai, Calcutta, Alexandra and Athens in 1930, he was the first Heath broker to visit the Far East. He was away six months, travelling by sea to visit the Excess Company's agents who in many cases had never seen an insurance man from London.

Another important link was forged when a young man named Robert Sprinks, then working as a surveyor for the Atlas company in Paris, came to London to try to place a difficult risk on Algerian cork forests. He had never been to Lloyd's, but after finding the way from the Bank station, he began to work his way steadily through the various Lloyd's brokers' offices in Lime Street. In one office he heard the comment: 'We'll never place it unless we can get Heath to lead it.' Further up Lime Street he heard the same words from another broker.

Sprinks decided that he had better learn more about this apparently all-powerful Heath. He looked up the name in the 'phone book, then found his way to Bankside House. Eventually he was seen by an underwriter who was sufficiently impressed by the quality of his detailed survey notes to take him out to lunch, and afterwards introduce him to Cuthbert.

Mr Sprinks still recalls how the great man studied his surveys with mounting interest, then gazed at him with eyes that pierced like gimlets. 'I've never seen survey work done like this. Have you ever thought of doing anything on your own?' It was the start of a long, fruitful partnership between Heaths and what is now, as the Groupe Sprinks, one of the most famous insurance firms in Paris.

Meanwhile America was still the brokers' land of opportunity. The Burning Cost scheme in particular provided new possibilities in almost every area of reinsurance. After Bagley's departure to Bowrings in 1928, Eric Squire had been sent to America with instructions to hold the Heath business against all rivals. His tour included not only the major insurance companies but also what were called the Factory Mutuals. Based on the old idea of people in the same line of business pooling their insurance risks, the Factory Mutuals, rejoicing in such names as the What Cheer? and the Firemen's Mutual, dated from the early 1900s.

On his 1928 tour Squire had been introduced to the president of one of the leading Factory Mutuals, and had tried to sell him excess of loss insurance. The president had not been interested. The Mutual's own resources, he said, were capable of dealing with

individual losses, for factories insured under the Mutual's scheme
were located far enough apart from each other for the chances of
more than one at a time catching fire to be remote.

By 1932, however, this situation had changed dramatically.
Fierce competition between the Mutuals and the companies
belonging to the Fire Insurers' Association had led the Mutuals to
add windstorm cover to their fire policies. Thus the catastrophe
element was brought in, for clearly a windstorm could sweep
through a whole state. Soon the Mutuals were clamouring for reinsurance in the London market, and premium flowed to Lloyd's.
(The new business was eventually to bring claims as well as premium. In the mid-1950s the Lloyd's market paid huge sums for the
damage caused by three hurricanes code-named Carol, Edna and
Hazel – underwriters wryly pointed out that the initials were familiar – which had boiled up in the Caribbean, then swept up the east
coast of America, where insured values were highest.)

One new area on the underwriting side was bank insurance.
Small local banks in America had become almost uninsurable
during the gangster age of the mid-1930s. But, as always in insurance, heavy losses pushed the rates up, and Heaths earned large
profits by coming into the market when it was rising.

Another profitable departure of the early 1930s was the pool
underwriting system known as Group 400/404. Stemming from
Heaths' unchallenged leadership on non-marine risks, the system
meant that a slip could be stamped by the syndicate on behalf of
several others, underwriting profits and claims being allotted on
a pre-arranged percentage. The system led not only to a stream-
lining and simplifying of underwriting methods. For Heaths themselves it was to mean increased income because the underwriting
on other syndicates' behalf was done on a fee plus commission
basis.

Meanwhile there was increasing tension between Heaths and
the Bain faction on the board in the mid-1930s. The difference of
view seems to have arisen over the question of whether or not a
lavish dividend should be paid on the company's shares. At a
board meeting just before Christmas 1934 it was decided to dis-
tribute a sum of £5,000 in the form of an interim dividend of fifty
per cent on the ordinary shares 'though a larger amount was
available and could have been paid'.

Evidently the Bains' view was that it not only could have but
should have been paid, for when the question came up again in
the following July, Cuthbert Heath referred to 'grave differences
between the parties' at the December meeting. He now proposed a
similar final dividend of fifty per cent, making a total of a hundred

A late photograph of Cuthbert sitting on board *Anne of Anstie* with Sarah and friends. The initials at the bottom of the photograph are written in Cuthbert's own hand

per cent for the year. This was carried, we are told, 'Sir Ernest and Mr John Bain dissenting' – though what the minutes do not tell is one of the most time-honoured anecdotes of Cuthbert, who was not above using his deaf-aid in Nelsonian fashion. When his proposal was put to the board, it is related, he switched off the deaf-aid while the Bains protested. When they had finished he switched it on again. 'That seems to be generally agreed then,' he is said to have observed benignly.

It is not the only story of his tactics with the deaf-aid. Lord Cobbold recalls 'being entertained by his technique with it. Though whether he used it because he wanted to shut off the opposition or because he was bored, I don't know.'

Though the Bain episode was thus clearly not the first time he had used the deaf-aid to such purpose, it was to be the last, for his days as chairman were now over. One of the most memorable pictures ever taken of him is a simple snapshot which shows him sitting in a deckchair on board the *Anne of Anstie*. There is still a dominance about his craggy features and huge frame, yet there is something about the photo which suggests that the giant's strength is ebbing.

Probably the picture was taken in the spring of 1938, shortly before he suffered the severe stroke from which he never in any

The swimming pool at Kitlands. Installed by Douglas Heath in the late 1890s, it was one of the first in the country

true sense recovered. After it he seldom moved beyond the grounds of Anstie. Clad in cap, scarf, and long Victorian travelling coat, he would be pushed in a wheelchair round the gardens by Daishe, his manservant. One of the effects of his stroke was that he was unable to move his head. His daughter Genesta was learning to fly at the time, and one of her sadder memories is of how she would circle the garden, practising navigation and 'waving the little plane's wings' to her father. He could not wave back, for he could not lift his head to see her.

Sometimes he was well enough to go out in the car for a short drive with George Salt, his faithful chauffeur. But gradually, and then more quickly, the use of his faculties was going. By the beginning of 1939 he could no longer speak or move out of bed. Daishe and George Salt took it in turns to sleep in the armchair in his room, and sometimes to read to him a little. The new young doctor from Holmwood, Dr Hal Boake, came to see him most days, but there was little that medicine could do. For six weeks he lay, silently gazing out over the view of his beloved downs towards Horsham. The room, Dr Boake recalls, was always full of geraniums brought in by Sarah.

But he was not to live to see the spring flowers. On 8 March, at nine o'clock in the morning, the long life which had caused such reverberations in the world flickered out with the quietness of a candle. Genesta, summoned home from Africa, arrived just too late to see him. Her aircraft had been delayed at Nairobi and she reached Coldharbour village just at the moment he died. It was as if, she thought, he had waited for her to be safely home.

That day he lay, almost in state, while the tenants, servants, and farm labourers who had also been his friends, filed slowly past his bedside. Three days later his ashes were carried on a farm wagon to Coldharbour church for his funeral service. The only flowers were from his garden, and the only sign that a notable man had passed were the two banners from his time as High Sheriff of the county.

In the more public world the death of the great underwriter was seen as marking the end of an epoch. The committee of Lloyd's took the unique step of holding a special meeting to record 'the high honour and respect in which he was held by the whole community of Lloyd's'. His was the first obituary in *The Times* on 9 March, with a reproduction of the Hay portrait. The *Daily Telegraph* carried a long article, and the *Evening News*, in an obituary of unaccustomed length for a businessman in a popular paper, told its readers that 'Mr Heath was generally given almost entire credit for the development of various forms of insurance undertaken by Lloyd's'. The *Economist*, a few days later, called him

> the first man to see the potentialities of insurance in the modern world ... There are few departments of our modern life which have not been touched at this point or that by his inventive genius. He had in him every element of greatness – intellect, character, vision, courage and a deep personal humility.

A memorial service was held at St Michael's, Cornhill, attended by almost every notable leader in the City. Many hundreds more recorded their sense of loss in the letters of condolence which poured in from America, from the Continent, and indeed from throughout the wide world in which he had helped business of all kinds to prosper. The letters recalled myriad innovations, new ventures, and all paid tribute to his personal attributes of courage and of kindness. Yet none of them, perhaps, summed him up as well as did young Dr Boake from Holmwood, who had never known him in his great days and seen him only as he awaited death in the flower-filled room at Anstie: 'He struck me as a very gentle person.'

CHAPTER SEVEN

The Modern Company

Cuthbert's death had not only coincided with the beginning of the war which was drastically to alter the physical and moral texture of the world as he had known it. It also meant the end of Heaths as it had been since the beginning, for until recently nobody had known a time when the master-underwriter's touch had not been, however lightly, on the tiller.

Moreover the next few years were to take their toll of almost all his old lieutenants. Montague Evans, who assumed the chairmanship on Cuthbert's death, himself died two years later. Arthur Burns had retired in 1938, and died in 1943. The only survivors of the early pioneering days were Merrick Tylor, who became chairman in 1941, Leonard Taylor, and Eric Irgens. From now on C. E. Heath and Co – the Bain connection had been broken off in 1936 with the resignations of Sir Ernest and his brother John Bain – would come to be increasingly in the hands of men to whom the founder seemed a remote and venerable figure.

The war itself was to impose considerable problems in the running of the office. Heaths' staff at the end of 1939 totalled 385, plus another forty already serving in the Forces. 196 members of the staff had been moved out to Staines, where Heaths had taken a block of flats named Riverbank, a sports pavilion, and a nearby Masonic hall. Between them the three buildings housed the accounts, American, and home departments. Because of the shortage of staff in wartime, local people were recruited for the less exacting tasks: one woman member of Heaths found herself sitting in the lounge of the Riverbank flats, initiating a retired gasmeter reader into the mysteries of American reinsurance.

During the war a notable step forward was made in staff relations. For some time the board had been considering means by which the staff might earn a share of the company's profits, and in 1943 they set up what was known as the Staff Trust Fund. Based on a loan of £87,000 from the company, it provided for the purchase of Heaths' shares, the income from which was then distributed annually to senior staff members. Largely the concept of the company secretary Robert North, it showed, as the 1923 Pension Fund had shown in its day, that Heaths were in the vanguard of schemes for their employees' welfare.

PREVIOUS PAGE The Zarate Brazo-Largo Bridge which spans the rivers Parana de Las Palmas and Parana Guaza in Argentina

Lloyd's itself continued to write business throughout the war years. Often there were formidable problems to be overcome, and one wartime device in which several of Heaths' staff played a leading part was the opening of BICO, the British Insurance Communications Office. BICO had a small office in New York for handling coded information relating to American risks being placed in the London market. George Thomson, who was in charge of the office in 1943, recalls that the origin of BICO was that,

> some of our competitors in the US wanted to use Britain's vulnerability as an excuse for getting us out of the way. They claimed that if details about, say, American ammunition plants or the movements of ships carrying vital goods between the United States and Europe were lying about in London when the Germans overran it, that information would be of great value to them. We said that it was perfectly possible to code the information so that it was impossible for the enemy to gain any knowledge from it. In the end it was so coded as to tell underwriters in London all they needed to know in order to continue to write the business.

The post-war period brought a more than usually large crop of interesting claims, including a sensational one when the Aga Khan was held up at gunpoint outside his Riviera villa. He had been driving out with the Begum when three men appeared, brandishing pistols. They had got away with £1¾ million-worth of the Begum's jewels, the insurance of which was led by Heaths in London. But as in the famous Cammi Grizzard case, the thieves seem to have lost heart, for a few days later a biscuit tin was found dumped outside a Marseilles police station. When opened, it was found to contain £100,000-worth of the missing jewels. Eventually about half the total haul was recovered, but the remaining loss was still one of the largest ever recorded in the history of jewellery insurance.

A less sensational but nevertheless intriguing case was that of a London diamond company whose policy excluded theft from an unattended car. One day one of the company's travellers, carrying a valuable package of diamonds, was going along the Dorking by-pass when he felt the need to find a convenient hedge. He noticed a handy place where he would be half-hidden, but from which he could still observe the car at a distance of about thirty yards. While relieving himself, he saw a man approach the car and proceed to break the window. Then, according to the traveller's story, the man took the package and made off in another car with an accomplice.

Leaving aside the coincidence that the thief knew the value of the package, Heaths' adjusters found, on going to the scene, that the traveller's account did not fit the facts. All that could be seen from the spot in question **was** the top of the car, which could easily have been broken into from the offside.

The Heath syndicate resisted the claim, and fought the legal case which followed on the ground that the car was unattended. They won the verdict – which was upheld on appeal – after a legal battle

An entertainer asked Heath to insure his monkey as being essential to his act. Heath thought, said 'Why not?', and issued the cover. Some years later, the monkey having died, the man returned to claim his money. The claim was settled in full and he left the monkey at Heaths who had it stuffed. It is now kept in their offices, an unusual example of 'salvage'

in which the counsel for the diamond company maintained that so long as the person in charge of a vehicle could see it, it must be considered as attended. Heaths' counsel's reply was that it was possible to be on the twentieth floor of a tower block and see your car being driven off. His view was accepted by the court, and the case helped to establish the point of law that 'attended' should mean an ability to prevent physical interference with the vehicle in question.

One very human story concerned the widow of an old country rector who was deeply distressed when she lost her engagement ring. Heaths paid her claim for £85, but six months later the old lady found the ring among her raspberry canes. She got in touch with her brokers, who told Heaths what had happened. The underwriters' first suggestion was that she might return either the ring or the money. This caused her a dilemma, for she had spent the money on a washing-machine, and she obviously wanted to keep the ring for sentimental reasons. Would the underwriters accept a washing-machine? The regretful answer was that most underwriters had one.

Meanwhile the view of the claims man on the syndicate was that a lot of assureds would have kept both ring and money and said nothing: the answer might be, he thought, to find a jeweller who would put an extremely low valuation on the ring, and then ask the old lady to pay this valuation. In the end such a jeweller was found, and the relieved old lady was told that the syndicate would be content with £35 – paid, if she preferred, by instalments.

Underwriters come across most aspects of the human comedy, from anxious old ladies to professional swindlers. One of the most remarkable insurance frauds of modern times was the famous Salad Oil scheme, the brainchild of an American named de Angelis. It hinged on the common commercial practice by which a merchant who has a valuable commodity which he is unable to sell immediately can raise money on it from a bank – the condition being that the goods are stored in an approved warehouse, and properly receipted.

This was the practice exploited by de Angelis in the Salad Oil fraud. He said he had large consignments of salad oil stored in what was known as a tank-farm, and on the strength of this he borrowed huge sums from not one but several banks – his only guarantee being the warehouse receipts which were signed by the man in charge of the depot.

But what the banks did not know was that this warehouse manager was an associate of de Angelis. Nor did they know that de Angelis had devised a simple method by which a small amount of oil in the tanks could be made to appear enormous. He had fitted a hidden tube into each tank so that, whenever a dipstick was inserted, it showed the tank as containing oil. The rest of the tanks were full of water.

When the fraud was discovered there were huge claims by the American banks, whose insurances covered them against losses caused by loans made on false or forged documents. For English banks, however, the policy wording referred only to 'forged' documents as opposed to 'false' ones, and when one English merchant bank put in its claim it was pointed out that the documents had not been forged – they had been issued in his own name by the warehouse manager who was de Angelis' accomplice. The merchant bankers' claim was accordingly rejected, but Heaths paid up on many others.

But from the 1960s onwards the emphasis was less on underwriting than on broking – a change that was symbolized by the appointment of Leonard Taylor, the first broker to become chairman, in 1950. Five years later he was succeeded by Charles Gould, who had been closely involved with Heaths' fortunes since before the Morgan Lyons takeover.

One reason for the new stimulus to the broking side was the expansion of Lloyd's worldwide business. Soon it was to be justified by more urgent reasons. In the days of the underwriter-chairman the role of the broker had been seen – as Cuthbert Heath had seen it more than half a century before – as being primarily to bring business to the syndicate. Even if the broking side did no more than break even, it earned its keep by helping the underwriting side to make substantial profits.

The complacent do not thrive for long in the insurance business, and this attitude was to suffer some startling setbacks in the 1960s. Dominating them was the famous Hurricane Betsy which swept through the southern states of America in 1965. Destroying homes and industrial premises on a scale unknown since San Francisco, one of the side-effects of Betsy was to teach a sharp lesson to world insurers. Rates for a long time had been too low, and the Lloyd's market in particular had for some years been content to rest on its underwriting reputation rather than the new forms of professionalism the market needed. Now, ruefully, the members of Lloyd's syndicates found themselves having to pay up on some uncomfortably large losses instead of, as usual, making a steady profit: the average loss per name for the year was £5,400.

Betsy was not the only problem faced by underwriters in the mid-1960s. There was the growing problem of inflation, and in the United States, escalating liability awards were beginning to put

Cuthbert Heath's Storm Register. Heath kept details about major disasters and based his rates on this information

			GALES													WINDS	
Observation Station	No. of Yrs obs.	No. of days gales for each month												Total Days gales	Av: No: Days per ann	No. Yrs obs.	mean Beau fort No. for Year	Re
		Jan	Feb	Mar	Apr	May	June	July	Aug	Sep	Oct	Nov	Dec					

Table 21. 112...

(5 inset)

TIDAL WAVE HAVOC.

MANY PERSONS KILLED BY TROPICAL STORM IN TEXAS.

D.C. 17.9.19

NEW YORK, Tuesday.

A message from Corpus Christi (Tex.) states that 15 to 20 people have been killed in a tropical storm. The damage is estimated at 1,000,000 dollars. Four thousand persons are homeless.

A score of people are drifting helplessly on floating debris in Corpus Christi Bay, and efforts were being made yesterday evening to rescue them.

The municipality is appealing for food. The town is without drinking water.

Virtually all houses on the Bay front and also boats were destroyed by a tidal wave. The floods are six to 12 feet deep in the streets.—Reuter.

£20,000,000 DAMAGE BY HURRICANE

MANY PEOPLE KILLED ON MISSISSIPPI COAST.

NEW ORLEANS, Oct. 2. '15

Communications now having been re-established, it is possible to ascertain the extent of the damage done by the recent hurricane on the Mississippi and Louisiana coasts.

One hundred and forty-nine people were killed, 106 others are reported dead, and 105 are missing. Hundreds of others are completely isolated by the floods. The damage to property is estimated roughly at £20,000,000.—Reuter.

A cable from Lloyd's agents at New Orleans reports that in the hurricane there the following casualties to shipping occurred :—

Four tugboats sunk.
Portuguese barque Santos Amaral sunk.
Seven vessels damaged in collisions, including the British steamer Hatumet.
Many small craft destroyed.

A number of vessels and two dry docks broke their moorings and were damaged. The Spanish steamer Mar Cantabrico, outward bound, went ashore below the city, but was assisted off and proceeded.

Another Lloyd's cable states that at Gulfport the British steamer Birchwood (light) and the British schooner Clara C. Scott are badly ashore.

CYCLONIC DISASTER IN UNITED STATES.

D.C. 1.5.24

Nearly 200 Victims; Scores of Buildings Blown Down.

ATLANTA (Ga.), Wednesday.

Tornadoes swept over three States in the south-eastern section of the country early to-day.

At the riverside mills, near Anderson, S.C., a mill and 50 dwellings were blown down.

Reports from various cities in the South show that altogether 47 persons have lost their lives, 130 are injured, and many others are missing.—Reuter.

TEXAS 6.5.1930 Tornadoes started in W. Texas, whirled fitfully across state, spreading death & ruin in its narrow paths. 84 lives lost: estimated damage £200,000. Damage worst at _Frost_ where 26 killed & entire business district demolished: School (frame building) torn to pieces: Railway Sta: disappeared & wreckage of goods vans scattered everywhere: ~~the more solidly built houses of wealthier res: cheaper dwellings blown away bit by bit~~ Reported 60% of city destroyed

Santo DOMINGO 3.9.1930 Hurricane, duration 4 hrs speed 150 miles per hr. reaching 160 record. 1000 killed, 2500 injured: nearly 5000 buildings destroyed: 29000 people homeless. British, American, Cuban, Mexican, Spanish, French & Haitian legations all demolished: a number of large buildings, including Bk. of Nova Scotia destroyed: also lunatic asylum & main cable office: the more solidly built houses of wealthier class were razed: cheaper dwellings blown away bit by bit. Reported 50% of city destroyed. Old churches withstood the storm.

Reuter's correspondent on horseback reached 24 mile beyond Azua: road impassable any further. Everywhere he found towns in ruins, bridges wrecked. Ruin fallen _LEEWARD ISLES_ also involved. considerable damage to houses of peasants: crops also extensively damaged. (See also note C)

P. T. O.

The liability and property insurance cover of the Port Authority of New York and New Jersey is placed in London by C. E. Heath & Co and includes the World Trade Center Complex

new pressures on casualty underwriters. Eventually the pressure of these events was to force insurance men to set their house in order, but in the meantime the obvious answer for Heaths was to make the broking side less subservient to the underwriting than it had been.

The new stress on broking had coincided with another important step in 1962. For some years Heaths' directors had been concerned by the fact that there were some very large private holdings in the firm, many of them in the hands of elderly people. The prices of the shares had become so high that few could afford to buy them, and there was a fear that, on the deaths of the present shareholders, control might pass into the hands of some rich outsider.

Therefore the decision was made that Heaths should take the

step of going public. In order to bring the price down, the shares were divided and reduced in their nominal value from £1 to four shillings. On the advice of their merchant bankers, Heaths decided to let the shares be quoted at £4, despite the misgivings of some of the board who would have preferred to see them quoted at £3. According to custom, Heaths' own staff were given a preferential chance of buying shares, though the board were at pains to point out that they should be regarded as a long-term investment rather than as a means of making rapid profits.

But the staff's keenness to have a stake in the company was immense. One city bank manager provided easy loans for members of the staff who banked with him to buy the shares, but the Heaths' directors, aware of the uncertainties of the stock market, continued to urge caution: one director recalls making strenuous efforts to dissuade an elderly woman on the staff from risking her life savings of £400.

But insurance shares in general were regarded at the time as being particularly desirable and 'the great attraction of this kind of share,' the *Daily Telegraph* told its readers in June, 'is that the investor can have a stake in the rapidly growing insurance business and at the same time avoid the risks which bedevil the ordinary insurance company.' Predictably, the million shares were over-subscribed when they came on the market on 2 July 1962, but before long it became apparent that Heaths had had the worst of bad luck in their timing. Within ten days of the new issue the stock market began to lose ground, and by the end of the month the shares had dropped to 62/-. By August 1963 they were still only 59/9 and eventually slipped to as low as £2. Later they climbed gradually, but it was not until the first bonus issue several years later that those who had bought the shares were to profit from them.

Another significant matter from the staff's point of view was the change made in the Pension Fund in April 1964. Since its inception in 1921 this had been run on a contributory basis – the employee contributing equally with the employer. Now, however, the whole amount was paid by Heaths. The £1¾ million assets of the fund were realized and the money paid into a new insured fund.

A more difficult problem was posed by the Trust Fund which, as we saw, had been set up in 1943 to give the staff a stake in the company's earnings. Now, twenty-five years later, the huge size of the Trust Fund – it comprised more than two million Heaths shares – had led to a situation where the payments had become part of the salary structure, containing no element of true bonus.

Moreover the Trust Fund was now working to the disadvantage of both parties. From the company's point of view, the introduction

of Corporation Tax in 1965 had meant that the Fund was costing
Heaths an extra £181,000 a year. But the major consideration was
that it was not helping the staff, whom it had been set up to benefit.
Since 1943 they had received payment in two different ways –
directly in the form of their salaries, and indirectly through the
Trust Fund. As the company's business had grown, dividends had
outdistanced salaries out of all proportion.

This might have been acceptable if there had been any link
between the Trust Fund and staff pensions, but there was no such
link. A man might be earning £1,600 a year from Heaths – £1,000 as
salary, and £600 from the Trust Fund. If his pension was calculated
on two-thirds of his salary, he would be very much the worse off,
for it would then be two-thirds of two-thirds, that is £666.

With all this in mind, plans were set in motion to wind up the
Trust Fund. Under the new arrangements, salaries were re-
structured so that the staff would not receive less than they had
previously been getting from both sources, and pensions were to
be related to the new consolidated salary scales. After much complex
discussion – the breaking of the Trust needed the approval of the
High Court and the written agreement of every single Heaths
employee – the new measures came into force on 31 December 1968.

By then Heaths had also become one of the first major brokers
to make a partial move out of London. In 1967 the lack of space in
Bankside House, plus rising costs, had led to a decision to acquire
an out-of-town office for those staff members who did not need to
work in the immediate area of the market. Because a large number
of employees were found to live north of the Thames, Southend
was selected as a site, and by the end of the year the company had
taken over a new building, Colman House, to house more than five
hundred claims and accounts staff.

Meanwhile the name of Cuthbert Heath continued to live on in
a special sense for those helped by the Centenary Fund which had
been set up by the committee of Lloyd's to mark the centenary of
his birth in 1959. The aim of the scheme, for which £140,000 had
been raised at its inception, was to provide bursaries at public
schools for boys whose parents would not otherwise have been
able to afford a private education. Six schools, chosen for their
proximity to London, and Cuthbert's own old school, Brighton
College, were involved in a scheme which in 1972 was adapted to
allow each school to claim an agreed sum from the fund and to
award bursaries at their own discretion.

A key relationship in Heaths' long history came to a somewhat
dramatic end at the beginning of the same year. For some time it
had been known that the Excess Company's underwriting reserves

Brighton College
today. The main
buildings are little
changed since
Cuthbert Heath's time

were not as large as they might have been, and now the company was looking for a means of improving its situation. On 2 February Dick Erlebach, who had become chairman in 1966, went round to Fenchurch Street to keep an appointment with Heaths' financial adviser John Gillam at Kleinwort Bensons, the merchant bankers.

When he got to the bank's offices Erlebach was greeted by a somewhat embarrassed Gillam. The meeting, he said, would have to be postponed because at the very moment discussions were going on with representatives of the Excess about their proposed takeover of Heaths. Kleinwort Bensons were in the awkwardly ambivalent position of advising both firms, and Gillam's proposal was that Heaths should seek advice from Barings. This was arranged, and over the next few days a series of hectically set-up board meetings and discussions took place.

These culminated in a summons to Erlebach and his deputy chairman, Frank Holland, from the chairman of Lloyd's, who at that time was Sir Henry Mance. Erlebach saw Sir Henry on the 10th, and was told that Heaths risked losing their position as an accredited Lloyd's broker if they were taken over: if a broker was acquired by an outside insurance company, the committee felt, there would be a danger of its getting and giving preferential treatment. Next day another meeting took place in the chairman's room at Lloyd's, this time with representatives of the Excess and both the merchant bankers. Sir Henry confirmed that Heaths could not remain Lloyd's brokers if they were taken over. Though Erlebach and the other Heath directors would have preferred to have fought the bid off on their own, the view of the committee had to be accepted.

The projected takeover thus came to nothing, and the historic special link with the Excess was now irreparably broken. Relations between the two companies continued, understandably, to be strained, and Heaths now decided to dispose of their £1 million holding in the Excess. Erlebach – as chairman of Heaths he was automatically a director of the Excess – resigned from its board within a few weeks. The Excess shares began to decline, and the company was itself taken over two years later by the American multi-national ITT, thus disappearing from this story.

All the same the very suggestion that they could be taken over – especially by what amounted to one of their own offspring – had been a blow to Heaths, and the whole episode now caused them to undertake a searching and critical self-examination. Until the end of World War Two, Heaths had been known in the market as the Rolls Royce of broking. Now, the impetus of the pioneering days was gone, and the name of Cuthbert Heath himself was no more than a legend in the market. The attitude within the office had become staid and sedate, going back to the time when it was said to be 'a privilege to be insured with Heaths'.

One effect of this was that in the immediate post-war period, Heaths had been overtaken by other brokers. In the past there had been few besides Bowrings and Willis Faber to present a challenge. But in the later 1940s and early 1950s the international broking business had expanded out of recognition. Firms like Sedgwick Collins, Bland Welch, Stewart Smith and Minets, which had been comparatively small before the war, now took off almost overnight, and the unpalatable fact was that Heaths were being rapidly outdistanced. 'There seemed to be no imagination at work, no thought given to expansion,' recalls one leading Dutch broker, Mr Marcel Kortenbout. 'One had the feeling that Heaths were always willing to see a client – provided he came to see them in their office.'

There were other, more practical factors which had a bearing on Heaths' declining fortunes. Promotion in the firm tended to turn on seniority rather than making sure the right man was in the right job, and at least one departmental head confessed to a sense of exasperation in the 1950s at the number of promising young people who departed to earn larger salaries at other brokers. The idea died hard that underwriting, as opposed to broking, was a gentleman's profession. 'If you were socially acceptable,' recalls one Heaths' director, 'you became an underwriter. If you didn't measure up you went on to the broking side.'

Clearly Heaths was in need of an injection of new ideas, and this was what now began under the direction of Dick Erlebach. Like most injections, it was not entirely painless. The weeks following the Excess affair were to bring a far-reaching programme of economies and retrenchment.

Erlebach had two formidable lieutenants. On the financial side he had brought in a high-powered young accountant, Michael Julian, to make a thoroughgoing analysis of the company's strengths and failings. On the broking side there was Frank Holland, who as a young man had been the first Heaths' broker after the war to be sent on an extensive US tour while still in his twenties, and who now as deputy chairman was a rising star in the Heath firmament.

The first step that Erlebach and his team took was to break down the firm's accounts on a departmental basis. Because the departments had been previously treated as a whole, there had been no indication of which were the profitable areas, and which were likely to be less so. When they were broken down, the management statistics revealed, startlingly, that only two departments, North

Frank Holland, the
Chairman of C. E.
Heath & Co Limited

American and International Reinsurance, had actually been making profits.

A more urgent, and in some ways more sensitive problem was posed by the board itself. One consequence of the unquestioned authority of Cuthbert Heath was that power in the company had always been vested at the top, with correspondingly less room for initiative from younger people. Now, without his personality to back it, the tradition still persisted.

The actual suggestion that there must be some reorganization of the board came in the first place from Frank Holland. At a board meeting within a week or so of the Excess bid, various people had put forward views. Then someone observed that Frank Holland had not been heard from. Holland's view had always been that 'there was a good company here if only we could get out from under', and he now told his fellow-members that if the company was to be subjected to a long hard look, the first people it should be directed at must be the board themselves.

The moment was a turning-point in the story of Heaths. Erlebach and Holland were commissioned to produce a new plan to be put before the board next morning. After working most of the night, the two came up with a scheme whose main feature was that the present board should be reduced from eighteen to a new holding

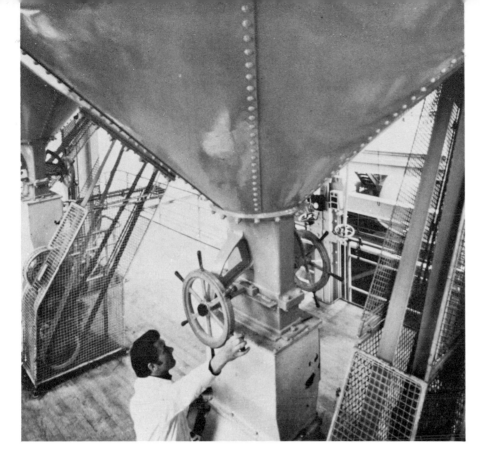

Adjusting the flow of malt and flaked barley to the mill at the brewery of Arthur Guinness Son & Co (Park Royal) Ltd. Heaths have been their main insurance brokers for many years

board of five. Most of those leaving the board were close to retiring age, but it says a good deal for their loyalty that the proposal was accepted without question.

The same pattern of slimming down was repeated elsewhere. Smaller and less profitable lines of business were cut out, and by means of early retirement rather than redundancies, the staff was cut from 1,050 to 750.

Following the revelations of the departmental statistics, there came a total replanning of the company itself. The underwriting side had already been hived off into a separate company, C. E. Heath and Co (Underwriting), and now a new company, C. E. Heath and Co (Insurance Broking) was created as an offshoot from the holding board. Planned to hive off the broking side in the same way as underwriting, it was linked in turn to a series of satellites – C. E. Heath and Co (Aviation), C. E. Heath and Co (International), C. E. Heath and Co (Marine), C. E. Heath and Co (UK) and so on. In the case of the UK company power was devolved still further to a series of domestic companies in the provinces and regions.

Thus the modern C. E. Heath & Co was born. The concept behind it was that those in charge of each company would be responsible to the main board for its successful operation: otherwise the way they ran their business would be left to them. Previously known as assistant directors, they now became full-fledged directors. The change of name not only gave a new sense of responsibility to the directors themselves. It was a significant gesture towards visiting foreign clients, who liked to feel they were dealing with someone of importance.

The point was perhaps a small one in itself, but it showed a new and more imaginative approach to the hectic task of winning business in a huge and highly competitive international market. Just over thirty years from the founder's death, the stage was now set for a return to the sense of initiative and expansion which had been his watchwords.

Anyone who is unaware of the contribution made by insurance broking to Britain's invisible exports would do well to study a very large green board on the wall of Heaths' North American department. On it are named in yellow letters the firm's largest US clients. The list ranges from Ford to the Port of New York Authority, from Greyhound to Gulf and Western. It includes travel companies, aeroplane manufacturers, generating stations, newspapers, the world's largest bridge and the only railway ever to have a song composed about it, the Atcheson Topeka and Santa Fe.

These large-scale risks come to London because no other market has such a reputation for expertise in large and complex kinds of business. But American brokers cannot come direct to Lloyd's: if they want to place a risk there, they must come through an accredited Lloyd's broker – a vital point which led, in 1978, to moves by several large US brokers to make more formal arrangements with their counterparts in London. Heaths, however, has so far remained independent of such links, preferring to rely on its reputation for skill and experience in North American business, and on its well-established contacts with American brokers such as Rollins Burdick Hunter. Heaths are in touch with Rollins every day by phone, and there are few working days in the year when there is not a Rollins broker visiting Heaths, or someone from Heaths in one of Rollins' sixteen offices in America. 'Each firm has had a significant effect on the success of the other,' says Rollins' chairman Adrian Palmer. 'Heaths and Lloyd's have played a large part in our becoming the seventh largest US broker.'

There are two words that more than any others define a modern broking business. The words are scale and speed – scale because of the size of the risks brokers are asked to place, and speed because the intense competitiveness of the modern market calls, more than ever, for quick responses. Only thirty years ago a broker would travel by sea and rail for three months at a time, often having to sit

The offices of C. E. Heath & Co in the Minories

up late into the night composing cables because few hotels then had telex facilities. 'In those days,' recalls Frank Holland, 'it was almost like an expedition. Nowadays a broker is more likely to go to New York one day and back the next in Concorde – often at a few hours' notice.' One recent example he cites came when Heaths' North American department had a call from a Philadelphia broker, one of whose clients was the Delaware River Port Authority. The broker had never done business with Heaths, but had heard they were particularly experienced in placing insurance on large bridges. Would Heaths be interested in calling when they next had a broker in Philadelphia, to discuss the business?

With true brokers' zest, Heaths decided to do better. They rang British Airways, keeping the Philadelphia broker on the other line. 'This was Tuesday,' recalls Holland, 'and the airline said there was a seat on Concorde on the Thursday. The North American department booked the reservation, then asked the Philadelphia broker if he could be at Dulles airport to meet their man at eleven on Thursday morning, preferably with the bridge authority people. The meeting took place, and the Heaths' broker returned by the same plane to London. The result was a multi-million dollar cover.'

If that is a fair example of speed, there are many more of scale. Today the placing of a single major international risk can take up the energies of more people than there were on the entire broking staff when the company was first formed. Heaths are reinsurance brokers for some of the largest petro-chemical complexes in Europe, and recently placed the reinsurance for the Salto Grande dam on the Argentine–Uruguayan border. Another still larger scheme for which they are involved in placing reinsurance is the Itaipu project between Paraguay and Brazil which, when it is completed in 1990, will be the largest hydro-electric scheme in the world, ten times the size of the Aswan dam in Egypt.

International business of this kind can come in two ways: either through local agents on the spot or by the setting up of local broking operations in which Heaths has a shareholding. In the case of the Salto Grande dam the contractor was Italian, the workforce Uruguayan, the equipment Russian – and the operation was made more complex still by the fact that under Argentine law, insurance must be placed with local companies, and reinsured with the state

The James Bay Hydro-Electric Project, Quebec. C. E. Heath & Co has arranged a major share of the builders' risk coverage for this multi-billion dollar project on behalf of a consortium of Canadian Brokers and ENCON

office. Such a situation will involve four stages – always in foreign
languages and often in a volatile political atmosphere. Heaths'
agent in the country concerned will tell them that the job is being
started, and they will then send someone out from London to see
the plans. He will be followed by an expert from London who must
be both a qualified engineer and a Spanish speaker. The initial
policy will be written by local insurance companies, who will then
reinsure with the state company. They will in turn pass on a large
proportion of the risk – in the case of the Salto Grande dam it was
ninety-five per cent – to the London market.

Oil exploration has brought new hazards and new opportunities
to the market. When oil was found at Prudhoe Bay in the ice-
wastes of North Alaska, Heaths placed the insurances for an armada
of tugs and barges which transported construction equipment –
including a pre-fabricated power station – to the site, which is
normally free from ice for only six weeks in the year. In 1975 when
the greater part of the equipment was ferried out, the ice-pack did
not melt till later than usual and the fleet of tugs had only approached to within one and a half miles of Prudhoe Bay when the
ice came back and trapped it. Engineers built a causeway of soil
and rubble from the oil terminal site to the boats – only to find that   Hurricane Betsy,
the giant 'crawlers' needed to carry the equipment had become   Florida, 1965

'Thistle A' North Sea oilrig under construction at Teesside

frozen to the decks. Undaunted, the engineers covered the fleet with hot-air balloons to thaw out the crawlers. The equipment was eventually landed safely – at an extra cost of $7 million.

Another unusual project was the insurance of the dock-gates built by John Laing at a Tees-side drydock during the construction of new rigs for the North Sea oilfield. Based broadly on the wartime Mulberry harbour, the concept involved a pair of floating concrete gates designed to protect the drydock from the sea. When one rig was finished, the water would be let in to allow the gates to be floated off for the rig to emerge. When it had done so, the gates would be towed back, ready for the building of the next rig. From the underwriters' point of view, the worst risk was that if for any reason the dock gates had failed to work, the sea would have come flooding in, wrecking the whole project, but despite the problems, Heaths managed to place the insurances for the construction of the rigs, the site, the equipment and Laings' liability for the construction – which involved putting together parts of the rig, made in many widely separate locations, with the help of the two largest cranes in Europe.

The story of the Middlesbrough dock-gates is one illustration of the classic ingenuity of the broker. Another is the high-risk area of helicopter insurance, where Heaths' pre-eminence is due to the skilful marketing of the Burning Cost insurance devised by Cuthbert Heath and Guy Carpenter in the early 1920s. The essence of the so-called Carpenter Plan, as we saw earlier, is that rates are calculated on the basis of previous claims experience: if future claims do not exceed an agreed figure, then the underwriter will take the business at a lower premium. The modern refinement of this is that the broker then places a second insurance with another underwriter, which covers the risk of the client's claim going beyond the first underwriter's figure. Thus, by spreading the risk the broker is able to secure a much lower total premium rate for his client.

But the scale of risks grows ever larger as, for example, in the insurance of the fleet of C. Y. Tung, one of the largest in the world today. Nevertheless what still counts above all is the quality of the broker's service to his client. Modern legislation has given employees many more rights than they had in the past, and it is part of the broker's task to point out to employers the kind of precautions they must instal in their factories under, for example, the Health and Safety at Work Act. Heaths' survey department is responsible for advising clients on these liabilities and on every other sort of loss prevention: a surveyor's daily work can range from advising the MCC on how best to safeguard the day's takings at a Test Match, to walking round miles of hydraulic cellars in the bowels of a South Wales steelworks.

It is the essence of the modern insurance scene that every client will have his special needs and special problems. For one client, The Stock Exchange, Heaths worked out a special policy covering errors and omissions by executives, infidelity and loss of documents. Public, as opposed to employers', liability is another problem: there was a very real risk of this sort for Laings, the contractors, when they came to place the cross on top of the newly-completed Coventry Cathedral. The only way to get it up was by using an RAF helicopter – and there was quite a possibility the helicopter might have dropped it on the crowds of people watching.

Despite its complexity and scale, most things in modern insurance still come back to Cuthbert Heath's classic pioneering and the precepts on which he worked. His presence noticeably lingers at the Heath non-marine underwriting box, where his 1906 earthquake book remains in use. The syndicate still leads most of the classes of business which he began, including consequential loss, burglary and jewellers' block, fidelity and earthquakes. Among the more recent innovations which he would, one feels, have applauded, are satellite and nuclear insurance. A Heaths underwriter insured the first space satellite against a failure to go into orbit, and the syndicate has been a leader in atomic energy risks since the 1950s. In reinsurance, too, Cuthbert's ideas echo almost uncannily through the market. Recently a reinsurance underwriter was looking for a way of keeping up the value of deductibles – the agreed first layer of any claim paid by the assured himself – which would offset the effects of inflation. Eventually he inserted an index-clause which related the deductible to changing money values – only to find that precisely the same thing had been done by Cuthbert as early as 1917.

Many innovations have come about as a result of building on existing policies: a recent refinement of consequential loss, for instance, is 'loss of accounts' insurance, which protects a business-man who loses his accounts in a fire and is thus unable to send bills out to get his money. Another new idea is a policy which covers someone building a factory against the possibility of work being interrupted if archaeological remains are found on the site where he is building.

It is in the nature of the insurance business that it can never stand still for long, and the expansion of the last seven years has stemmed from a determination that the company should learn from past errors and not rest on its achievements. In line with this belief, the 1970s have seen a variety of new departures, among them the acquisition of the Groupe Sprinks subsidiary in Paris, seen as a major step towards the growing EEC markets. In London the Lloyd's underwriting operation has been augmented by the setting up of an agency company which writes in the London market on behalf of overseas principals in America and for a time, Scandinavia. These have included two American companies, Bellefonte and Pinetop. Bellefonte is owned by Armco, among its other activities the world's third largest steel producer, and Pine-top by the huge Greyhound conglomerate.

Another example of the complex ramifications of international insurance is the formation of two groups in the Far East. One, a joint venture with Rollins Burdick Hunter and the Dutch brokers, Hudig Langeveldt, began in 1959 when the joint company of Heath Langeveldt Ltd set up its first office in Singapore. A Kuala Lumpur office followed in 1962, one in Bangkok in 1965, and another in Hong Kong six years later. In 1974 the enterprise was strengthened still further by the inclusion of Rollins Burdick Hunter, who,

Heaths' creative approach is reflected in the advertisement of the Company's Financial results which won *The Times Grand Prix*

The Heath report

The insurance world of C.E. Heath.

American Airlines
The London Market placement for American Airlines Inc. is arranged by C. E. Heath for Alexander and Alexander N.Y.

Port Authority of New York and New Jersey
C. E. Heath has placed in London and world-wide markets the liability and property insurance cover of the Port Authority of New York and New Jersey including the World Trade Centre complex.

Cartier
Cartiers are one of the leading International Jewellers with branches in the major cities of the world. A large part of their insurance requirements and those of other major jewellery concerns are handled by C E Heath in the London and Overseas markets.

The Thistle A Project
World's largest off-shore platform – the Thistle A project. We were chosen by the contractors, Laing Offshore, to insure the site : the dock gates ; certain equipment used in the construction of the platform including the specially adapted cranes and their transportation and erection ; plus their overall liability for Laing Offshore in their capacity as contractors.

Cuthbert Heath House
The Group's new headquarters building was officially opened by the Chairman of Lloyd's, Sir Havelock Hudson, on 17th September 1976.

Sir Havelock Hudson remarked that in his book on Lloyd's, Eric Gibb wrote **"** There are today few Lloyd's Underwriters who business has not been revolutionised by what Cuthbert Heath did : and to his imagination and foresight even the insurance companies owe much of their present prosperity **"**

Sir Havelock Hudson went on to comment **"** I have, during my period of office, tried to get across to the public, to politicians and to government officials, the enormous and highly successful efforts of Lloyd's Brokers in travelling the length and breadth of the globe to bring back business to the London Insurance Market.

Lloyd's Brokers contribution to the U.K. economy cannot be over-emphasised and no small part of that contribution comes from C. E. Heath & Co., a great Lloyd's firm **"**

Another outstanding year Group profits up 80%

Highlights from the year to 31st March 1977 shown in the Report and Accounts and the Statement by Frank Holland, Chairman of C. E. Heath & Co. Limited

The Year's Results
The excellent progress made in recent years has been maintained. The operating profit at £11,454,000 shows an increase of almost 80% over the previous year and the profit available for appropriation at £5.76m is up by 90%. In this context it is interesting to note that the group was recently included in the Financial Times List of major quoted companies (market capitalisation above £10m) as the second best performing company in terms of growth in market capitalisation for 1976.

A final dividend of 14.0p gross – the maximum permissible – is recommended and in addition the Board recommend a capitalisation issue of two new shares for every one held. This issue will help to correct the balance between our general reserve and the capital of the company and should also improve the marketability of our shares.

Insurance broking
The continued progress of our insurance broking operations is most heartening. Every operating division has made a significant advance in spite of market difficulties. Notwithstanding the obvious problems associated with devaluation of sterling, especially as it affects Lloyd's capacity, our experience in placing covers throughout the international insurance and re-insurance markets in the last year has, if anything, added to the total capacity available.

The Group now handles insurance premiums amounting to £310 million through its broking operations.

Underwriting
The Lloyd's Underwriting operations for the 1974 Account resulted in a substantial loss for our Non-Marine Syndicate and there is no profit commission contribution from this source. Our Agencies company is continuing to develop with the introduction of the Pine Top Insurance Company, and the increased volume being written by the Bellefonte Insurance Company has enhanced the fee income of the company in Australia. The revision of our operating basis has taken place and the continued growth of these operations reflects the very great contribution of our staff there.

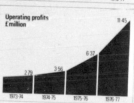

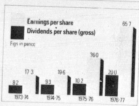

are contin...
Australia will continue...

Future prospects

It is unrealistic to expect the rate of growth achieved in the last few years to continue, especially if the pound achieves greater stability against other currencies. However, in the past year we have obtained a significant amount of new business and I see no reason why we should not continue to build on our firm foundations.

Satisfying the insurance requirements of our major corporate clients in the past year has been a challenge to our marketing skills. Our success gives me confidence that we shall continue to be recognised as having special strength in this area of vital importance to industry.

Although the 1975 Lloyd's Underwriting Account will almost certainly produce a small loss, a return to profitability should follow shortly. I am also hopeful that our Agencies company will produce a healthy contribution to our results.

Overseas we are looking for continued growth particularly from both our Australian operations – Broking and Underwriting.

Frank Holland

Copies of the full Report and Accounts are available from the Secretary.

C. E. Heath & Co. Ltd.

Cuthbert Heath House, 151-154 Minories, London EC3N 1NR
Tel. 01-488 2488. Telex: 885280   888088.
INTERNATIONAL INSURANCE BROKERS
REINSURANCE BROKERS AND UNDERWRITING AGENTS

Although the size and complexity of the risks insured have grown, the perils of the sea are as relevant today as when Cuthbert Heath first started as an underwriter

like Heaths, had long-established contacts with the Amsterdam firm. Today the firm of Heath Langeveldt Rollins owns eight broking and two underwriting companies. Another Rollins-linked company was formed in 1974 when Heaths acquired half the shareholding in a company previously jointly owned by Rollins and the Rockefeller company, Ibec. Now renamed Rollins Heath Inc., the company has offices in Tokyo, Yokohama, Seoul and in South America.

Perhaps the most significant of recent worldwide developments has been in Australia, which produces the largest profits of any of Heaths' international operations. In 1971, Heaths acquired an insurance company in New South Wales called Industrial Liability Underwriters, and since then has acquired or formed three others. There are underwriting rooms in Perth, Adelaide, Hobart and Geelong as well as Melbourne. The main company has now expanded into fire, accident and marine, and in 1978 it launched out for the first time into motor business.

One effect of the need for scale and speed is that broking houses themselves have become enormous – indeed some of the mergers between London and American brokers produced, in 1979, the

The Australian
insurance broking
subsidiary of C. E.
Heath handles
insurance for the
Mount Isa Mines,
Australia. When
completed, the lead
smelter stack on the
right will be 270 metres
high – the tallest
structure in the
southern hemisphere

term 'mega-broker'. But despite the expansion of the last few years,
the company has remained faithful to Cuthbert Heath's belief in the
individual, to the concept that insurance in the end comes down to a
conversation between two people, and that it is the quality of the
individual broker or underwriter that matters. 'The genius of
Lloyd's,' sums up the company secretary Brian Thompson, 'is that
people are encouraged to be true to themselves and so you get an
originality and freshness of approach. You don't get many grey
people in Lloyd's: they are positively black and white, and this is
what makes it all so fascinating. This is the Lloyd's that Cuthbert
knew – and why he would still find himself at home in the company
today, despite all its changes.'

In the days of Cuthbert Heath insurance companies used to pride
themselves on the kind of solidity and substance that was measured
in terms of mahogany doors and palatial boardrooms. Since 1976
most of Heaths' broking staff have been housed in relaxed open-
plan offices in the Minories where one is aware of no such status
symbols. In the small downstairs boardroom the most cherished
exhibit – next to the Orpen portrait of the founder – is the Queen's
Award for Export Achievement which Heaths won in 1978. Close

Cuthbert Heath House in the Minories. An impression by Martin Kawala of how the new building will look when completed

Heaths marine box. The company broke with its long, exclusively non-marine tradition when it reopened a marine underwriting syndicate in 1979

beside it is another prize – *The Times* Grand Prix awarded for the best financial advertising in 1977. Heaths nowadays are firmly aware of the importance of keeping their name before the public: one recent venture was their sponsoring of the *Heath's Condor* yacht which was first home in the 1977 Round-the-World race. It was a marine enterprise which one feels Cuthbert Heath himself would have approved – just as he would have liked to know that, ninety-nine years after he himself began as a marine underwriter at Lloyd's, another wheel had come full circle. In January 1979 the Heath syndicate broke with the non-marine tradition of more than seventy years to re-open a marine box in the Room.

So, after our brief glimpse of the modern company which is his legacy, we come back to Cuthbert. Not indeed that we have ever left him for long, for the pride the company takes in its founder remains real, vivid and as intensely personal as if the young men in the company today had actually known him. 'For anyone under forty,' said one director, 'there's nothing more irritating than to be told how old so-and-so would have done it. But the one man I wish I'd known in this business is Cuthbert Heath. I wish he was around today. From all I've heard, he'd have cut through the problems.'

It is one of the characteristics of a great pioneer in any field that one cannot easily imagine what the world was like before him. Today neither the individual nor the great multi-national company can move a step without insurance. The exporter must insure against his overseas customers failing to pay up. The individual must insure his house, his car, his valuables. None of this would have been possible without the innovations recorded in these pages. The insurance industry has produced many people of talent, intelligence and drive, but only one man of influence who has actually changed its history.

Insurance is nowadays not only more widely understood than ever before. It is the object of a huge and growing public interest. Whenever some major disaster or new enterprise flares across the world headlines like a comet, there is also the comet's tail. Whether it is terrorist damage in Beirut or Belfast, or the construction of a power station in the Arabian Gulf or of an oil terminal in the Arctic Circle, there is an insurance aspect to attract public interest.

Scarcely a century ago insurance had no such relevance to the world around it. True, there were companies who insured the public against fire risks and underwriters who wrote marine risks. But the huge field of liability, where a man is rightly held to be answerable to his neighbour, was as yet unthought-of, and vast numbers of other risks went unregarded. When Cuthbert Heath came to

Lloyd's, it was a mere underwriters' club, and one of dwindling importance. When he left it, it had become the world's most comprehensive market.

His principles of probity and integrity are no less important than his innovations. Cuthbert Heath once said that he had gone into insurance because it was a way of making money that did not hurt anyone, and throughout his life he worked in terms of the understanding that lay behind a policy, not merely its strict wording. A broker once came to him and said that he accepted there could be no claim under a particular policy, because the point in question was not covered. Heath's reply was that the person who had taken out the insurance had intended to be so covered – and the claim was paid. Another time he told one of his staff that the insurer's job was 'to get a man out of trouble. That's what he's paid you for.' The phrase is not only an embodiment of what insurance is about. In a consumer age, it is a precept which the industry forgets only at its peril.

In the end it was Lloyd's that he loved, and his living monument is the great non marine market of today, where a host of brokers place the world's risks and so help industry to prosper. Today it is of far greater significance to Lloyd's than the once dominant marine market, and its scope and influence are continually growing.

But in the long run his name and achievements deserve to be remembered on a wider canvas. The story of Britain's mercantile achievement since the Industrial Revolution is very much the story of her pioneers: of such men as Arkwright, Brunel and Stephenson who found a gap in the state of human knowledge or enterprise in their time and went on to fill it, enriching society in the process.

To their names might be added that of Cuthbert Heath, the courteous giant of insurance.

The Room at Lloyd's
with the Loss Book in
the 1880s

Illustration Acknowledgements

Figures in **bold** type indicate pages opposite which colour plates are to be found.

The following abbreviations are used:
CEH: C. E. Heath & Co Limited
CM: Photo Christopher Mikami
GLC: Greater London Council Photograph Library
Guildhall: Guildhall Library, City of London
ILN: *Illustrated London News*
Lloyd's: Courtesy of Lloyd's of London
MEPL: Mary Evans Picture Library
TRC: Courtesy of the Three Rooms Club, Lloyd's
V & A: Victoria & Albert Museum, London

The publishers would like to thank the following for permission to reproduce illustrations, and in particular to Christopher Mikami who photographed most of the originals.

Reverse of Frontispiece The Times
Frontispiece CM
6-7 Barnaby's
11 *The Graphic*
12-13 National Trust
15 Lady Claud Hamilton
17 Lady Claud Hamilton
19 Lady Claud Hamilton
20 Mrs Joan Sarll
21 Mrs Joan Sarll
22 CEH
25 Post Office Copyright Reserved
27 (*left*) Mark Heath Esq
27 (*right*) Lady Claud Hamilton
30 ILN
31 ILN
32 Lady Claud Hamilton
33 Mark Heath Esq
34 ILN
36 Brighton College
37 Brighton College
38 Mark Heath Esq
40 (*above*) Guildhall
40 (*below*) Photo John Mikami Esq
41 (*both*) CM
41 *The Graphic*
42-3 Guildhall
44 *The Graphic*
45 Guildhall
46 Guildhall
47 Guildhall
48 *The Graphic*
49 *The Graphic*
50-1 *The Graphic*
53 Lloyd's
54 Guildhall
55 *The Graphic*
57 Lloyd's
58 Lloyd's
59 *The Graphic*
60 (*both*) Lady Claud Hamilton
61 (*above*) Lady Claud Hamilton
61 (*below*) CEH
63 Photo Science Museum, London
64 MEPL
66-7 GLC
69 Popperfoto
70 Lady Claud Hamilton
71 CEH
73 MEPL
76 V & A
79 CEH
80 Mrs Lee Steere
82 Lady Claud Hamilton
85 Lady Claud Hamilton
86 TRC
89 ILN
91 Broadwood Trust
92 Lady Claud Hamilton
94 Popperfoto
96-7 Imperial War Museum
101 Lloyd's
106 CEH
111 CM
112 Lloyd's
113 (*above*) Lewis Angel Esq
113 (*below*) TRC
116 Mark Heath Esq
119 Lady Claud Hamilton
120 Lady Claud Hamilton
125 Lloyd's
126 Imperial War Museum
127 Guildhall
129 Popperfoto
132-3 National Motor Museum
138 Lloyd's
140 Port Authority of New York and New Jersey
141 (*above*) Surrey County Cricket Club
141 (*below*) EAST Lines Ltd/WTO Inc.
142 TRC
143 Excess Insurance Company
145 Guildhall
146 TRC
148 Popperfoto
152 Mrs Lee Steere
153 TRC
154 Mansell Collection
155 CEH
158 TRC
159 Lloyd's
160 Evergreen Helicopters Inc
161 CEH
162 (*both*) Mrs Joan Sarll
164-5 French Tourist Office
167 Mrs Joan Sarll
168 Mrs Joan Sarll
170 Mrs Lee Steere
171 Mrs Joan Sarll
172 CEH
174 Popperfoto
175 News of Industry Ltd
181 Mrs Joan Sarll
182 CM
184-5 Courtesy of INDER
188 CEH
191 CEH
192 Port Authority of New York and New Jersey
195 Brighton College
198 Trevor Humphreys
199 Arthur Guinness Son & Co (Park Royal) Ltd
201 CM
202 Society of Energy, James Bay
203 Keystone
204 Laing Offshore Contracts
207 Walter Judd Ltd
208 Keystone
209 M.I.M. Holdings Ltd
210 (*above*) CEH
210 (*below*) CM
212 CM

Index